Lasting Learning Press

Study Smart: 10 Ways to Master the SAT/ACT Using the Science of Learning

By Nicholas C. Soderstrom, Ph.D.

Foreword by Robert A. Bjork, Ph.D.
Distinguished Research Professor
University of California, Los Angeles

Praise for *Study Smart*

"In *Study Smart*, Soderstrom has delivered a tight, witty, and precise guide to studying that makes accessible a century's worth of authoritative, if often arcane, research. It's the kind of book that is more than useful; it keeps you company. I wish I had that company in some of my lonelier moments preparing for the SAT and other intimidating tests."

— **Benedict Carey**, author of *How We Learn*

.

"*Study Smart* brings the science of learning out of the lab and into the hands of parents and students. I wouldn't want to face the gauntlet of standardized tests that students do without these techniques in hand. Too often studying *harder* is mistaken for studying *smarter*. *Study Smart* guides students to use their time more productively by revealing scientifically-validated but unintuitive methods for enhancing learning, memory, and understanding."

— **Aaron S. Benjamin, Ph.D.**, Professor of Psychology
at the University of Illinois at Urbana-Champaign

.

"*Study Smart* is an instant classic: simple, accessible, and packed to the gunnels with the best cognitive psychology has discovered about how we learn and remember. If all students, teachers and parents knew and understood the straightforward but counterintuitive strategies contained in this entertainingly-written little book, we might just herald in a learning revolution. Highly recommended."

— **David Didau**, author of *What If Everything You Knew About Education Was Wrong?*

.

"A *great* test prep book that gives you immediately useful insights based on sound science. This book will not only help you master the SAT/ACT—it will also help improve all of your learning."

— **Barbara Oakley, Ph.D.**, author of *A Mind for Numbers* and co-instructor
of *Learning How to Learn*, the world's most popular online course

.

"Easy to read and easy to use, this book will prove an indispensable guide for students preparing for the SAT/ACT *and* for students seeking to maximize their GPA while minimizing their study time."

— **Daniel T. Willingham, Ph.D.**, Professor of Psychology
at the Univeristy of Virginia and author of *Raising Kids Who Read*

"Students believe that their scores on standardized tests are relatively fixed, but their performance can be improved via the evidence-based study strategies explained so well in this book. The strategies can also be used for learning more broadly, too."

– Henry L. Roediger, III, Ph.D.,
James S. McDonnell Distinguished University Professor of Psychology
at Washington University in St. Louis and co-author of *Make it Stick*

.

"Dr. Soderstrom has written a marvelous book, *Study Smart*, which reviews the approaches to learning that show the most promise toward the development of an ideal training program for mastering challenges, such as the SAT and ACT. The book is one of the most readable efforts I have come across in my 40 years of work in various learning domains."

– Francis J. Pirozzolo, Ph.D., former Chief of the Neuropsychology Service at Baylor
College of Medicine and founding editor of *Developmental Neuropsychology*

.

"This book can help make motivated students more efficient learners. The often unintuitive learning strategies that take center stage in Study Smart are presented in a very accessible form, and thus this book can help students of all ages learn how to learn. Study Smart lays the groundwork for applying the science of learning to enhance the entire learning process."

– Alan D. Castel, Ph.D., Associate Professor of Psychology
at the University of California, Los Angeles

.

"Anchored by the science of learning, this book provides an admirably accessible and cutting-edge guide for how students can effectively study for the SAT/ACT. An invaluable bonus is that these techniques will help learners navigate learning challenges at any level to make learning stick."

– Mark A. McDaniel, Ph.D., Professor of Psychology
at Washington University in St. Louis and co-author of *Make it Stick*

.

"Your brain is a learning machine, and as with any machine, it helps to have an instruction manual. Soderstrom has given us precisely that, in the form of this simple, powerful, and useful set of rules and tips that will benefit *students, teachers,* and *parents* alike."

– Daniel Coyle, author of *The Talent Code* and *The Little Book of Talent*

" **You learn
to speak by speaking,
to study by studying;
in just the same way,
you learn by learning
how to learn.** "

— Tom Mecklen

© 2016 Nicholas Soderstrom and Lasting Learning, LLC.
All rights reserved.

No part of this publication in print or in electronic format may be reproduced, stored
in a retrieval system, or transmitted in any form or by any means, electronic, mechani-
cal, photocopying, recording, or otherwise, without the prior written permission of the
publisher.

The information in this book is furnished for informational use only, is subject to change
without notice, and should not be construed as a commitment by Lasting Learning LLC.
Lasting Learning LLC assumes no responsibility for any errors or inaccuracies that may
appear in this book. The views expressed in the book do not necessarily reflect those of
any agency or institution.

Design by Clement Mok
Published by Lasting Learning Press, Lasting Learning LLC

Library Congress Catalog No.
ISBN 978-0-9976280-0-5
First Printing: June 2016

TABLE OF CONTENTS

Foreword: i
The Increasing Importance of Knowing How to Learn
Robert A. Bjork, Ph.D.

Acknowledgments   vi

Introduction:
Learning Doesn't Work the Way You Think It Does   1

Chapter 1 | Develop a Growth Mindset
Learn how to see every challenge as an opportunity   8

Chapter 2 | Put Yourself to the Test
To learn more, get tested more often   26

Chapter 3 | Space It Out
How to use the "spacing effect" to get a higher score   42

Chapter 4 | Mix It Up
Alternating what you study helps you learn better   56

Chapter 5 | Keep It Fresh
For lasting learning, change up where and how you study   74

Chapter 6 | Explain Yourself
Why learning to ask "why?" and "how?" matters   92

Chapter 7 | Teach It to Learn It
To raise your score, don't just study a subject, teach it   112

Chapter 8 | Look Back to Move Forward
How to raise your scores through self-reflection   128

Chapter 9 | Imagine That
*Ancient memory techniques you can use today to
raise your scores*   140

Chapter 10 | Visualize Your Path to Success
*Practical visualization techniques that will help
achieve your learning goals*   154

Notes   170

FOREWORD | Robert A. Bjork, Ph.D.
The Increasing Importance of Knowing How to Learn

This book summarizes, in a uniquely concise and readable way, what the science of learning has to say about how to study and learn effectively. The specific mission of the book is to pass on that information in the form of advice to students who want to optimize their preparation for, and performance on, an important test, the SAT (Scholastic Aptitude Test) or the ACT (American College Testing) in particular. From a broader perspective, though, the benefits of drawing on the information in this book in order to study smarter for the SAT or ACT go well beyond increasing one's score on either of those specific tests. Making a serious effort to draw on and understand the research findings presented in this book constitutes an exercise in a critical life skill: learning how to learn.

Knowing how to learn effectively has always been important, but never more so than now. Our complex and rapidly changing world requires that we acquire new skills and knowledge, or update old skills and knowledge, and often on our own. More and more learning is happening outside of the classroom, not simply during the years of formal education, but across our lifetimes as our jobs, careers, interests, and hobbies change. Happily, the opportunities to learn on our own are increasing as well: computer-based technologies provide new opportunities to learn on our own, sometimes as an adjunct to formal education, but often outside of formal education.

The bottom line is that knowing how to learn effectively has never been more important and the opportunities to do so have never been more available. What the last several decades of research on the science of learning have demonstrated, though—as is summarized so effectively in this book—is that it is not an easy matter to become an effective learner. Becoming a maximally effective learner requires engaging in activities that often go against one's intuitions, violate some standard practices in education, and/or create a sense of difficulty.

How we learn versus how we think we learn
During the last several decades, research on learning has been accompanied by a growing body of research on related metacognitive processes—that is, research on how we *think* we learn. Such research has examined, among other things, learners' beliefs about how learning happens; learners' judgments of the extent to which some to-be-learned material has been learned and will be recallable later; and learners' judgments with respect to how and when to-be-learned material should be studied, including judgments such as deciding what to-be-learned materials need more or less studying, when one can stop studying, and so forth. Overall, this research has revealed that there is frequently a striking mismatch between the instructional conditions and activities that enhance long-term learning versus the activities that learners *think* enhance learning—or engage in simply as a matter of habit.

The need to embrace difficulties and challenges

One reason there is such a mismatch is that conditions of study or practice that are maximally effective in terms of fostering the understanding of to-be-learned material—and increasing the likelihood that material can be recalled later—often create a sense of difficulty or challenge. Carrying out the most effective learning activities can reduce the amount of time spent studying as well as produce greater learning, but such activities involve our active, not passive, involvement and require that we contend with challenges.

In short, as Elizabeth Bjork and I emphasized in a brief article addressed to students, becoming maximally effective as a learner requires "making things hard on yourself, but in a good way."[1] The "good way" of "making things hard on yourself" refers to incorporating activities that create what I called "desirable difficulties," which are conditions of learning or practice that create challenges for learners and appear to slow the rate of learning, but then enhance long-term retention of to-be-learned knowledge and skills.[2] Such activities include—as summarized and illustrated in this book—spacing rather than massing repeated study sessions; interleaving rather than blocking one's study of separate topics; varying how to-be-learned material is studied and interpreted; and using self-testing, rather than restudying, as a learning event. We need, in summary, "to be suspicious of the sense of ease and undeterred by the sense of difficulty."[3]

Bringing the right state of mind

Basically, as learners we need to keep our eyes on the prize, so to speak, which means achieving a level of learning that results in durable and flexible access to to-be-learned knowledge and skills. Doing so, though, requires not only knowing about the activities that create durable and flexible learning, but also bringing a kind of tenacity to the task, fueled by a belief in the remarkable capacity we all have to learn. As is stressed in this book, for example, learning effectively requires—among other things—embracing, not avoiding, errors; adopting a growth mindset;[4] and envisioning a path to success. This short book constitutes a guide to actually taking that path.

ACKNOWLEDGMENTS

This book would have been impossible to produce without the help and dedication of several individuals. I wish to personally thank Sam McMillan for helping me write this book, Clement Mok for providing the design and planning work, and Cameron Broumand for his support throughout this endeavor. I am indebted to Robert Bjork—who has been an incredible mentor to me—for writing an insightful foreword. I also extend my gratitude to the following individuals who took the time to review this book: Aaron Benjamin, Benedict Carey, Alan Castel, Daniel Coyle, David Didau, Saskia Giebl, Mark McDaniel, Barbara Oakley, Fran Pirozzolo, Henry Roediger, and Daniel Willingham. Finally, I would like to express my appreciation to the learning scientists around the world whose research has revealed the beautifully sophisticated nature of human learning and memory.

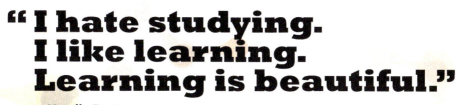

"I hate studying.
I like learning.
Learning is beautiful."
— Natalie Portman

Introduction

Learning Doesn't Work the Way You Think It Does

There's nothing easy about the SAT/ACT. Hours of sitting. Hundreds of questions. And it seems like your entire future is riding on it.

If you are looking for a sneaky way to game the SAT/ACT, keep looking. This book won't help. You won't find a strategy to guess the order of multiple-choice questions. There's not a practice problem in sight.

But if you are looking for a book that will help you learn the fundamentals of how to study for the SAT/ACT (and just about anything else you'll ever need to learn), this is the book for you. In clear, simple terms, *Study Smart* will explain break-throughs from the science of learning—and how you can use them—that will change the way you study forever.

There are plenty of books that promise to help you ace the SAT or ACT, or reveal their secrets. Here's the real secret: learning is unintuitive. It doesn't work the way you think it does.

Many of the strategies outlined in *Study Smart* revolve around a rather strange idea: when it comes to learning, making things hard on yourself can be a good thing. Durable, flexible learning often requires that we follow the path of more resistance. To make learning last, make it *more* difficult. But not too difficult.

By slowing down the process of learning—that is, by putting up roadblocks, interrupting the process so it doesn't flow smoothly, and studying the "wrong" way—long-term learning improves. One of the world's leading learning scientists, Dr. Robert A. Bjork, who wrote the foreword to *Study Smart*, calls these counterintuitive techniques "desirable difficulties."[1]

Let's define desirable difficulties. They are conditions of learning that slow down short-term performance but actually enhance long-term learning.[2] Desirable difficulties pose challenges for the learner that need to be overcome. But in overcoming those challenges, lasting learning occurs. In other words, when it comes to learning, short-term pain often leads to long-term gain.

Decades of scientific research suggest that introducing difficulties during the learning process can raise recall, improve retention, and sharpen motor skills.

When it comes to learning new information, I've included some desirable difficulties that make studying slightly harder in the short run. Follow the techniques in *Study Smart*, use them in your study practice, and you'll get powerful, measurable improvements in the long run. Here are just a few techniques that you'll learn more about, and be able to use, thanks to *Study Smart*:

The smart way to use tests

Most people hate tests, but did you know that tests are actually powerful learning tools? In Chapter Two, *Put Yourself to the Test,* you'll learn that tests are your friends... if you know how to use them. It turns out that taking a test forces you to retrieve information from long-term memory. Instead of just measuring what you know and don't know, test-taking also strengthens your memory and improves learning in a huge way.

A spaced out way to study

All-nighters are a terrible way to study. But we've all been there and done that, studying the material again and again for hours on end, in the hope that something will stick. Then we rise at dawn, take the test at 8 a.m., and a week later, poof, the information is gone. Cramming, also called "massing," might help in the short run, but it's a poor way to learn.

In Chapter Three, *Space It Out*, you'll learn that it's much better to break up your study sessions into short, manageable chunks. By interrupting ourselves and spacing out what we learn (and thus making learning more difficult), we can actually improve our long-term abilities. Rather than reading a single chapter five times in one day, use spacing to your advantage by reading the chapter once a day for five days. You'll have spent the same amount of time learning the subject, but your long-term mastery will skyrocket.

Better learning is in the mix

Instead of studying one topic at a time before moving on to the next topic, there's a more effective way to learn. It's called "interleaving," and as I explain in Chapter Four, *Mix It Up*, it means mixing up the topics you want to learn. By alternating the topics you study, you make the learning process a bit more difficult, but you also make your learning last longer.

Let me illustrate this principle with an example from the world of sports. Imagine you want to work on your golf game. Most of us would go to the driving range and hit a bucket of balls, one drive after another. Then we might head over to the practice green and practice putting for an hour. Learning scientists call this "blocked practice," and it's everywhere. However, as study after study suggests, a much better way to improve your golf game would be to mix up your practice sessions such that you go back and forth between driving and putting. The same thing is true in school. When studying for your geometry class, instead of practicing volume problems over and over, mix up volume problems with area problems. It might seem strange and it cuts sharply against our common sense, but it works.

Learning is best served fresh

One of the first things we were taught about how to study—by our parents and our teachers—was to find a quiet place to study and then stick with it. The science of learning says this is exactly wrong!

As I'll show you in Chapter Five, *Keep It Fresh*, you should change up where and how you study to improve your retention. By varying the learning conditions, you link your memories with a wider range of cues that can help trigger your memory later.

Much of what you know about learning is wrong

If you've read this far, it should be obvious that a lot about how people think learning works is dead wrong, and that we have to overcome our preconceptions in order to optimize our learning. And I'm not just pulling this out of thin air. There is plenty of science to back this up. In fact, most of the techniques I suggest in this book— and those discussed at length in several recent books on the science of learning[3,4,5]—are based on research that dates back decades.

In *Study Smart*, we'll dip into the research that explains why these techniques are so effective when it comes to strengthening our learning. Best of all, you'll discover lots of practical, simple-to-use study methods you can use today to help you prepare for the SAT/ACT.

If you are reading this book, congratulations. You've taken the first step to studying smart. Instead of a silver bullet, you'll find silver buckshot. Ten-plus chapters loaded with scientifically-validated techniques that can improve the way you study and boost your scores.

Ready for more? Begin with Chapter One, *Develop a Growth Mindset.* You'll learn how facing the challenge of studying for the SAT/ACT with a positive attitude can prime you for success.

Now turn the page and let's *Study Smart.*

1

Develop a Growth Mindset

Learn how to see every challenge as an opportunity

There's nothing easy about the SAT/ACT. But having the right mindset can make things easier. Basically, a mindset is your belief about yourself and your abilities. It's a way to frame your view of the world. And the view you adopt for yourself is one ingredient that can impact your performance on the SAT/ACT, not to mention your life—the way you lead it and the person you want to become.

You've probably heard your friends say "I'm not good at learning new languages" or "I'll never get algebra." That's an example of what psychologists call a "fixed mindset." People with fixed mindsets believe they are born with an innate, natural talent. Or lack of it. When they encounter hard problems at school, they may not work hard because they think they can't improve. Even worse, they may avoid challenges because they worry they'll make mistakes and look dumb.

At the other end of the scale is what Stanford psychologist Carol Dweck calls a "growth mindset." Students with growth mindsets tend to think intelligence can grow over time, with hard work and study. When these students work on challenging tasks, the struggle to master the subject becomes an opportunity for growth. If they fail, they see each slip-up as a result of a lack of effort, or maybe not having the right skills. So they try harder or they learn the skills they need to be successful.

More challenge, more fun

Who would want to do the same puzzle over and over again? That doesn't sound like much fun. Turns out, kids with fixed mindsets tend to do the same puzzle over and over because they like to know they will get it right. Kids with a growth mindset often do a puzzle once and then look forward to the next, harder challenge.

Mindsets make a difference

Having the right mindset can impact the outcome of your effort. In her book *Mindset: The New Psychology of Success,* Dweck reports that effort plays a crucial role in learning. People with a growth mindset think that qualities such as intelligence, creativity, and athletic ability can be improved through effort and developed over time. They believe the cards they are dealt represent a starting point, not a dead end. As a result, a growth mindset can foster a passion for learning that can last a lifetime.[1]

Here's the truth about your mindset: by embracing challenges, you have the potential to get better at just about anything, even the SAT/ACT. But remember: having a growth mindset is just one ingredient in the recipe for success. Being motivated to learn and using effective learning strategies are also critically important.[2]

Two kinds of mindsets:
the story of two report cards

Dylan gets a D in algebra. His classmate, Dakota, also gets a D in algebra. While no one sets out to earn a D in math, that bad report card can either serve as an indication of failure or lead the way to further growth. And that can depend on your mindset.

Dakota, who has a fixed mindset, sees her grade as a sign that she's no good at math. In fact, she decides she'll never be smart enough to do well in school. You can imagine how that negative mindset will impact the rest of her school year.

Dylan, who has a growth mindset, believes that working hard will help him learn more and achieve his goals. In other words, he knows failure isn't a permanent condition. He believes that the more you work at something, the better you become at it.

Dylan sees the D on his report card as an opportunity to study harder, or figure out a different way to learn the subject. He gets a tutor. As a result, Dylan's intelligence grows. And when he retakes the test, his achievement scores increase.

You can apply this same positive attitude to the SAT/ACT. When you get the results back from your PSAT or your first SAT/ACT, use them as a guide on how to improve your score when you take the test again. Once you know what your weaknesses are, with the right mindset and practice, you can get to work on building skills in that area.

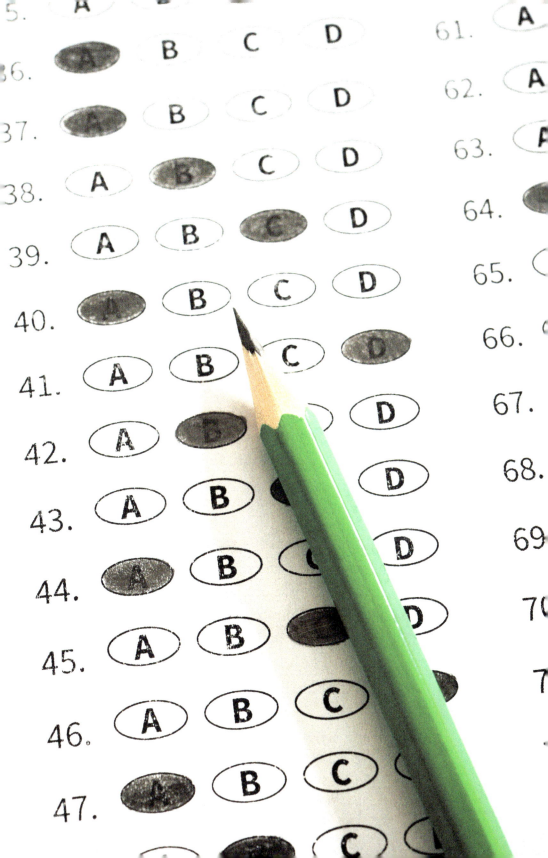

Does it work?

Will a positive mindset improve your ability to learn and achieve better grades in high school? A team of psychologists from Stanford University and the University of Texas decided to study just that.

These psychologists knew that mindset matters most when students encounter obstacles, so they focused on students who underperformed. They looked at about 1,500 students who had trouble learning in 13 different high schools across the United States.

Here's what they did: in each school, they taught three 45-minute classes on how to adopt a growth mindset. The basic message in each class was that by taking on ever more challenging problems, we exercise our brains the same way a weight lifter exercises his or her muscles. The students in these classes learned that their intelligence can grow—that is, they can actually get smarter—when they work hard on challenging tasks.

The researchers discovered that the students who took the growth mindset classes were "more likely to earn satisfactory grades in core academic classes."[3] In other words, when students learned that intelligence can grow over time with effort and practice, their grades improved.

A for effort: grit matters

Call it determination. Call it passion or perseverance. But the ability to work toward long-term goals, no matter how much you fail, is a huge predictor of your ability to learn, achieve, and be successful—not only in school, but in your work and life.

Angela Duckworth, a psychologist at the University of Pennsylvania, studied West Point cadets, kids at the National Spelling Bee, and even teachers in really tough schools. She wanted to find out what separated those who succeeded from those who did not. Turns out, the single factor that predicted success wasn't GPA, it wasn't IQ, and it wasn't natural ability or talent. The one factor the successful people shared in common was grit: the ability to work toward a goal, stick with it, and not quit.[4]

And the best way to build grit is to adopt a growth mindset.

Here's the good news: when it comes to mindsets, you have a choice

When it comes to doing well in school, it helps to have an off-the-charts IQ. But there's a way for the rest of us to start down the path to success, too: develop a growth mindset. And here's the good news: a growth mindset can be learned.

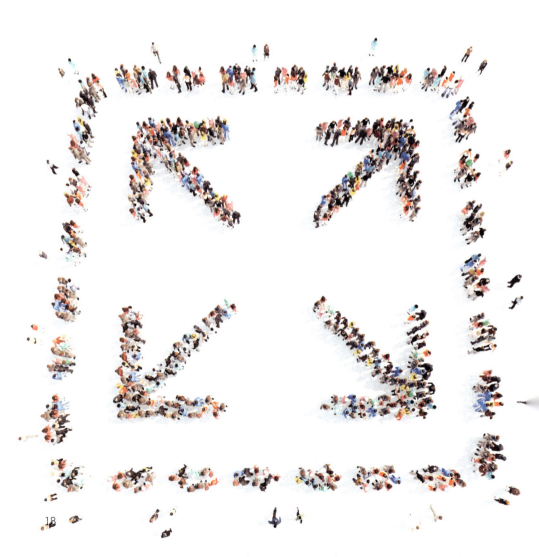

Carol Dweck, the psychologist from Stanford, says you can actually teach yourself to adopt a mindset that turns each new obstacle you face into an opportunity to learn.

Dweck suggests there are practical steps you can take to adopt a growth mindset:

Make the choice
First, she says, when it comes to adopting a growth mindset, you have a choice. Instead of approaching a challenge with a fixed mindset, Dweck says you can choose to take on the challenge with a positive attitude. By embracing the challenge as a chance to stretch your ability, you can improve your ability to learn.

Try harder
A challenge demands we ramp up our effort, Dweck says. When the going gets tough, people with grit get going.

Learn from failure
See your mistakes as problems to be solved, not failures.

Focus on the process
If you want to become a high achiever in school, focus on the process, Dweck suggests. Then develop effective strategies for tackling tough problems. This could be as simple as joining a study group, working with a tutor, or even taking a remedial class.

Hear criticism
Then realize you can take action to make improvements.

For parents:

a smarter way to praise

An effective way to develop a growth mindset in your kids, according to Dweck, is to stop praising their natural abilities. Kids praised for intelligence (that is, for being "naturally smart") become reluctant to take on more challenging tasks, for fear of looking dumb. Eventually, their performance on tests can begin to suffer.

In Dweck's research, she discovered that the students who were praised for their innate smarts wanted easy problems to work on. But students who were praised for their hard work wanted more difficult problems to work on, so they could challenge themselves to learn more.[5]

Dweck actually studies how the stories we tell our kids can make a difference in their academic performance. Her suggestion: tell your children stories about people who worked hard and overcame obstacles to achieve great things. Instead of "Mozart, boy genius," tell your kids how Thomas Edison tried 9,000 times to make a light bulb until he discovered a way to make it work.

Take charge of your learning

When it comes to learning, the most important thing to learn is that you are in charge. You have an incredible capacity to learn anything you put your mind to. Instead of backing away from schoolwork, take on the tough classes, and dig in. You can master the SAT/ACT if you put in the time and effort it takes to succeed.

Yes, with each passing year schoolwork only gets harder. But it gets harder for everybody. With a growth mindset and the right type of practice, you can develop your intellectual abilities. When you see each new challenge as a chance to learn new things, you'll enjoy school more and improve your grades. Even better, with a growth mindset, you begin to see learning as fun!

You can use a growth mindset to define success, too: it's not always about a grade. It's about working hard to become your best.

"By seeking and blundering we learn."

– Johann Wolfgang von Goethe

TAKEAWAYS:

The brain is a learning machine.

Your brain is like a muscle. It responds to exercise. Faced with difficult problems, the brain grows, reorganizes itself, and literally learns to learn.

You can grow your intelligence.

You can start down the path to becoming smarter with a growth mindset and a desire to learn.

Embrace challenges.

Hard work, taking on challenges, and coping with obstacles improves your ability to learn.

You are in charge of your learning.

You can choose to adopt a growth mindset and see challenges as opportunities to learn.

Failing is a part of learning.

When you encounter a setback, try to understand what went wrong and how you can get better. Instead of thinking you are a failure, try a different learning strategy, take a remedial class, work with a tutor, or sign up for a test prep service.

Mindset matters, but so does practice.

A growth mindset is just one ingredient in the recipe for success. As you study for the SAT/ACT, be sure to engage in the learning strategies discussed in the rest of this book.

Notes:

What steps will I take to develop and sustain a growth mindset?

Put Yourself to the Test

To learn more, get tested more often

Let's say you just studied vocabulary words for the reading section of the SAT/ACT. What would lead to better learning—studying all of the words again or testing yourself on what you studied? The science of learning says that testing, or "retrieval practice," is a much more powerful way to learn, especially if you want to remember something for the long term.

Most of us think of testing only as a way to measure what we've learned. But decades of research by learning scientists have shown that testing actually improves our ability to learn new information. Because taking a test forces us to retrieve the answers from our long-term memory, testing actually strengthens that memory. It's called the "testing effect," and it's a powerful way to learn new things.

Learning to love the test

Most people hate tests. Teachers think it's a pain to give them. Students dread them. But here's why you should love getting tested: taking a test helps you learn.

Quite simply, if you get tested on a subject and you recall it successfully, you will remember it much better in the future than if you had never been tested at all. Psychologists at Washington University in St. Louis showed the power of testing as a learning tool. They tested 120 students on their ability to remember a reading assignment. After an initial reading of a passage on general topics like the sun and sea otters, students either reread the material or took a test on it. Then, the students returned for a final test five minutes, two days, or one week later.

After five minutes, students who reread the assignment did a little bit better than those who took the test without getting a chance to reread the material. But here's where things get interesting. After two days, the pattern reversed: the students who were tested remembered more than those who reread the passage. After a week, the results were even more pronounced. The students who reread the passage remembered only 42 percent of the material. The students who were tested remembered 56 percent of what they read. In other words, taking a test after studying led to much better long-term retention.

The same psychologists wondered if rereading the material over and over again might make a difference, so they tested that, too. The results are surprising. In their experiment, one group of students studied a short passage during four study periods. In all, they read the passage about 14 times. Another group got to study the material during three study periods and then took one practice test that did not provide any kind of feedback about their performance. They were able to read the passage about 10 times before the practice test. And finally, one group studied the passage during one study period and took three follow-up tests. That group read the passage about three times before the practice testing started. A week later all three groups were tested to see how much of the passage they remembered.

Study less, test more

The students who read the passage 14 times recalled 40 percent of the material. The students who read that passage 10 times but were tested once recalled 56 percent of the material. But best of all, the students who read the passage only three times but were tested three times recalled 61 percent of the material.[1]

The more the students read, the more they forgot. The more they were tested, the more they remembered. That's because the process of retrieval makes the material stick in the mind. And, in a variation of "practice makes perfect," because students were getting tested so often, they actually developed their test-taking skills. That's a powerful learning technique.

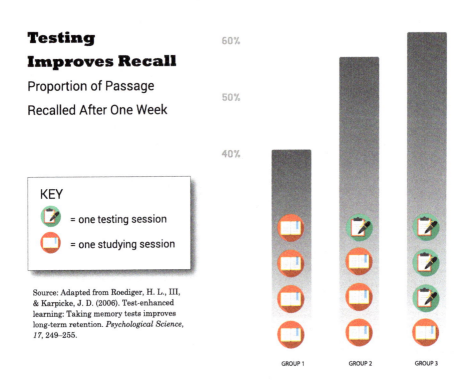

Testing Improves Recall
Proportion of Passage Recalled After One Week

KEY
= one testing session
= one studying session

Source: Adapted from Roediger, H. L., III, & Karpicke, J. D. (2006). Test-enhanced learning: Taking memory tests improves long-term retention. *Psychological Science, 17*, 249–255.

GROUP 1　GROUP 2　GROUP 3

Read it and forget it.
Test it and remember it.

It sounds exactly backwards, but the effects are so powerful, I have to repeat them here. Nearly a century's worth of research has shown that taking tests can boost learning significantly more than simply reading something over and over again. As you practice for the SAT/ACT—no matter what section—remember to test yourself as you go. If you want to learn something, test yourself on it!

The right schedule improves results

We know that testing forces our brains to retrieve information, and that builds learning because it requires more effort and taps long-term memory—the very type of memory that is needed come test time for the SAT/ACT.

But what type of testing schedule should we use? Well, psychologists have studied that, too.

In a study conducted in the late 1970s, researchers tested students' ability to remember names. Each student was given a deck of cards with each card containing fictitious first and last names. During the study phase, students flipped through the cards at a nine-second rate, during which time they studied and practiced retrieving the names in various ways. Thirty minutes after the study phase, a final retention test of all the names was given. The researchers discovered that the most effective retrieval schedule during the study phase was one where the retrieval attempts of the names were spaced out with increasingly longer time intervals between each attempt. They called this "expanding retrieval." In other words, learning was better when each successful retrieval attempt was more challenging than the last one. In fact, the expanding retrieval schedule produced nearly 100 percent better recall than when the names were only studied and never tested during the study phase.[2]

Expanding the gaps between your tests forces your brain to work harder to find the right answer, which makes learning more durable if you succeed. As a bonus, you can introduce more and more new material into the gaps as they get longer and longer.

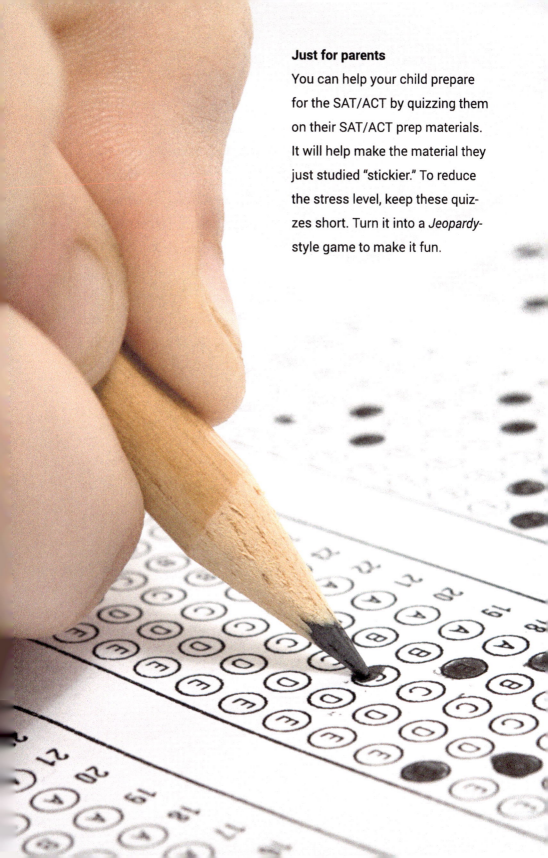

Just for parents

You can help your child prepare for the SAT/ACT by quizzing them on their SAT/ACT prep materials. It will help make the material they just studied "stickier." To reduce the stress level, keep these quizzes short. Turn it into a *Jeopardy*-style game to make it fun.

Does it work?

Scientific American reported the results of frequent testing on 1,400 students at Columbia Middle School in Illinois. Students in social studies and science classes were divided into two groups. In one group, teachers presented the material once and the students reviewed it three times. In the second group, the material was presented once and the students were quizzed on it three times. Results: at the end of the semester, the students who took more frequent tests scored an A- compared with the C+ achieved by the students who reread the material.[3] Which would you rather have on your report card at the end of a semester?

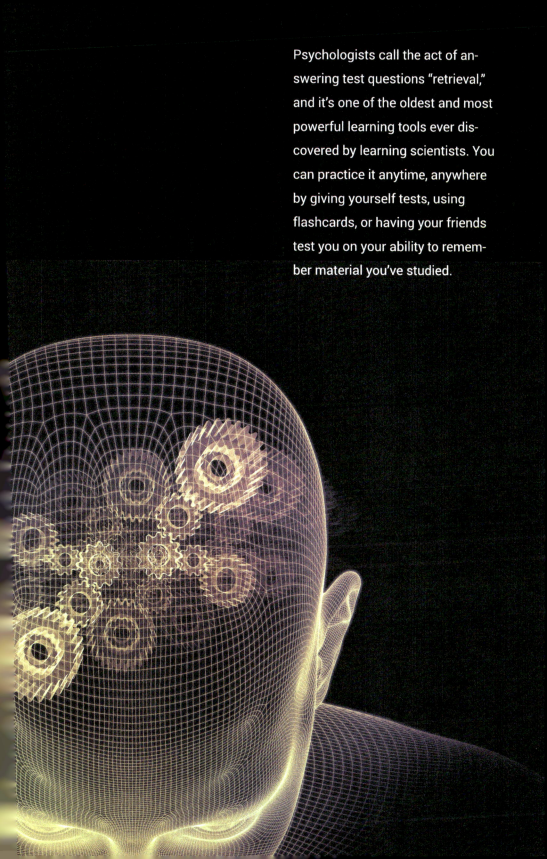

Psychologists call the act of answering test questions "retrieval," and it's one of the oldest and most powerful learning tools ever discovered by learning scientists. You can practice it anytime, anywhere by giving yourself tests, using flashcards, or having your friends test you on your ability to remember material you've studied.

" **Testing leads to failure, and failure leads to understanding.**"
— Burt Rutan

Pretesting helps future study

Imagine taking a test *before* you had a chance to study the material? That would be a guarantee of failure. No one would want to do that.

Except taking a test beforehand can help you learn more material in future study sessions. Educators call this "pretesting," and it could be an effective technique for improving your results on the SAT/ACT.

UCLA psychologist Elizabeth Ligon Bjork and I decided to test the effectiveness of pretesting in a classroom of Bjork's own students. Before the start of some of her lectures, we tested her students, giving the class a short pretest on topics that were to be discussed in the lecture that came immediately after the pretest. Even though the students bombed the pretests, we found that performance on the final exam was about 10 percent better for pretested topics than non-pretested topics. One idea for why pretesting boosts learning is that it primes people to pay better attention when the material is presented later.[4]

"Learning is not attained by chance, it must be sought for with ardor and attended to with diligence."

— Abigail Adams

TAKEAWAYS:

Do it often.
The more you test yourself, the better the results. Testing yourself after you study is critical to improve your learning. There are lots of practice SAT/ACT tests out there, including full-length practice tests—take them!

Prime your brain with pretesting.
Test yourself on a topic before you start studying it. It might seem strange, but take some practice SAT/ACT tests before you dive into the material.

Write it down.
If you use flashcards as a study aid, write down the answer first, then flip the card over. You'll remember better and learn more.

Make it harder.
Don't look up the answers in a textbook or on Google. Instead, force yourself to remember it. Recalling the answer—that is, retrieving it from long-term memory—improves learning. And the harder it is to retrieve the answer (provided you can retrieve it), the better.

Expand your schedule.
To make retrieval harder, use an expanding retrieval schedule by increasing the gap between tests.

Notes:

How will I use testing, or retrieval practice, to boost my learning?

Space It Out

How to use the "spacing effect" to get a higher score

To study smarter, space out.

That's the message from educational researchers who study how we learn. Their work reveals that by breaking up the material to be studied—that is, spacing out the study sessions—you'll learn more and retain it longer. It's called the "spacing effect." So, instead of cramming as much information into your head the night before a test—the way most students study—do yourself a favor and spread out the material you want to study again over several sessions. It's a powerful and incredibly easy way to improve your test results on your SAT/ACT.

100 years of remembering

Learning and memory scientists have known about the spacing effect for a long time. Over 100 years ago, a German researcher named Hermann Ebbinghaus conducted experiments on himself to learn how memory works. In one experiment, he tried to memorize a series of nonsense syllables—like *DAX, BOK,* and *YAT.* For some of the syllables, he studied them over and over again on the same day. For others, he spaced his study sessions apart over several days.

Ebbinghaus discovered that he could retain a lot more information when he spaced out his study sessions—studying a little bit every day—rather than studying a lot of information in one day.[1] Here's the good news: you can use the same technique to improve your score on the SAT/ACT.

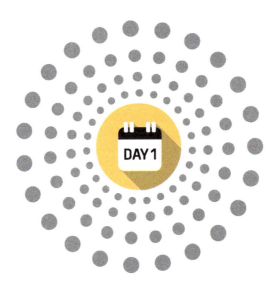

More recent research backs this up. In 2011, thanks to a schedule change at their university, researchers were able to test the spacing effect in their classes. In two different statistics classes, the same amount of material was taught in a two-month class and in a six-month class. This meant the students in one class were forced to cram more studying into a short period of time. Meanwhile, students in the second class spaced out their studying over a longer period of time.

When they received their grades, students in the six-month class outperformed students in the two-month class. Even though they studied the same amount of material for the same amount of time, the students whose study sessions were broken apart over a longer schedule did better. On a final exam that tested their conceptual understanding, students in the six-month class scored 36 points compared to only 23 points for students in the two-month class.[2]

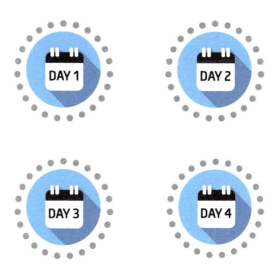

Why it works

Scientists studying memory have several theories on why spreading out practice sessions works better than cramming. Some researchers think that when you space sessions too close together, your brain doesn't have to work very hard to retrieve items from memory. To make matters worse, the ease with which you remember something can fool you into thinking you've actually learned it. In other words, learning a subject by repeating your study in back-to-back sessions can be counterproductive.

Another theory about spaced practice sessions involves reminding. Repeating the study session a second time serves to remind you of what you studied during the first session. By doing this, you retrieve the material from your memory, which enhances your learning. To see how retrieval can boost learning, take a look at Chapter Two, *Put Yourself to the Test*.

A third theory researchers point to is called "consolidation." Each time you study something it builds on the first session, leaving a trace stored in your memory. The second time you study the same material, it benefits from the trace memory you've already established. By spacing your study sessions over days, weeks, and months, you consolidate all those trace memories. Spacing your study gives your brain the time it needs to stabilize the material in your long-term memory. So when the SAT/ACT rolls around, you'll be able to recall information easier, thanks to the strength of the memories you've built up over time.

Strategies for smarter studying

Instead of cramming for the SAT/ACT, space out your study sessions. Learn a bit of the material at a time, every day. As an alternative to five hours of cramming for a test in a single session, try to review the material for one hour a day for five separate days. You'll spend the same amount of time studying, but you'll get better results when you space out your study sessions.

5 hrs.

1 hr.   1 hr.   1 hr.   1 hr.   1 hr.

How it works

To remember it, forget it. Just a bit. You would think that when it comes to studying material, the less you forget, the more you can remember. But research on students who were asked to learn translations of Spanish turns this theory on its head. After an initial study session, students were given six separate review sessions to learn the translations. In one group, students learned the Spanish words back to back, with no spacing between sessions. As you might expect, they learned the translations quickly, showing almost perfect accuracy by the sixth session.

A second group learned the Spanish translations in six practice sessions spaced one day apart. With just one day between sessions, they had little chance to forget what they learned. As a result, after six days, their test results were almost perfect, too.

Finally, a third group of students learned the Spanish words in six sessions spaced 30 days apart. That's right, each study session was separated by an entire month. Because the time period was so far apart between study sessions, forgetting was much greater. Students' initial test scores after the sixth session were much lower than those in the other groups.

But here's where things get interesting. Thirty days after all six sessions were completed, each of the three groups was tested one last time. The students who retained the most information were the ones who spaced their study sessions 30 days apart. In other words, the spaced practice sessions were the most effective. And the longer the interval, the greater the benefit.[3]

Spacing works

Researchers who study memory and learning have tested the spacing effect on kids as young as two years old, elementary school students, high schoolers, college students, even people in senior living communities. Across all ages and subjects, studies consistently show that breaking up your learning across several study sessions improves your ability to remember it for longer periods of time.[4]

Learning takes practice, forgetting happens fast

Unless you practice your learning, you'll forget it. That's why cramming won't work. To prepare for the SAT/ACT, schedule your study sessions over a period of days, weeks, and months.

**"Tell me and I forget.
Teach me and I remember.
Involve me and I learn"**

– Benjamin Franklin

TAKEAWAYS:

Stop cramming for tests.
Studying lots of information in a short period of time leads to rapid forgetting, even though it might feel like you've learned a lot.

Time is on your side.
To study smarter, schedule your study sessions further apart. Inserting time in between review sessions will help the information stick in your memory.

Spacing reinforces verbal learning.
Spacing your study sessions in intervals of a day or two is a powerful way to learn vocabulary words as you prepare for the verbal portion of the SAT/ACT.

Build a study schedule.
To build a useful practice schedule, start with the date of your upcoming SAT/ACT, then work backwards to schedule plenty of study sessions that are spaced apart. Mastering the SAT/ACT takes some planning.

Notes:

How will I plan my study schedule to take advantage of the spacing effect?

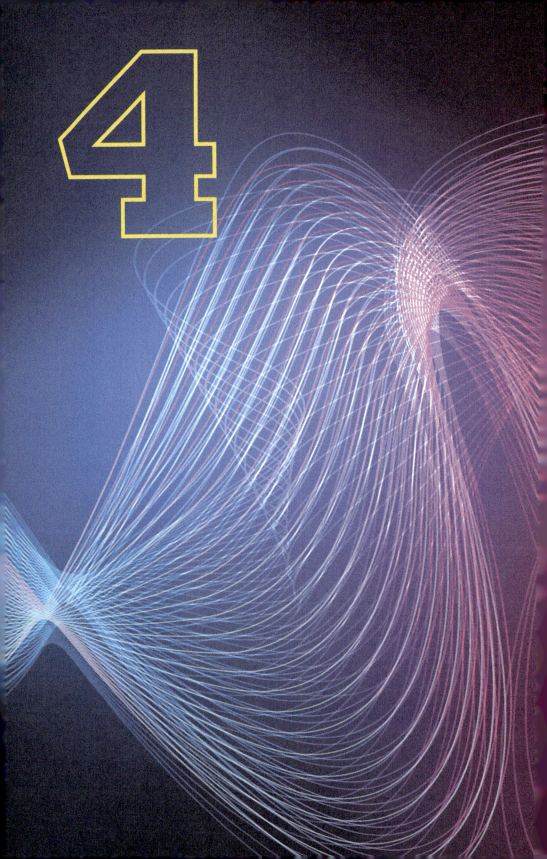

Mix It Up

Alternating what you study
helps you learn better

To master a subject, mix it up. That's the advice of scientists who study how we learn. Their research indicates that instead of drilling down on a single topic at a time, we learn better when we mix up the problems we study. Researchers call it "interleaving." It's an incredibly easy technique to use, and can be especially effective when it comes to preparing for the SAT/ACT.

Batter up

To understand how interleaving works, imagine a baseball player taking batting practice. He's got 45 practice swings. He could choose to swing at 15 fastballs in a row, followed by 15 curveballs and 15 changeups. Repeatedly practicing the same thing over and over again is a technique called "blocked practice." Alternatively, our batter could take 45 cuts at fastballs, curveballs, or changeups coming at random. That's called "interleaved practice," and I just described a real experiment that was conducted with college baseball players.

To determine the practice schedule that worked best, after six weeks of batting practice there was a final test. The batters attempted to hit all three types of pitches without knowing the type of pitch in advance, just as they would need to do in a real game. The batters who interleaved their practice improved their hitting ability by 56 percent. The batters who blocked their practice improved by 25 percent.[1] That's a powerful lesson for baseball players who never know what pitch is coming next. It's also an effective study technique as you prepare for the SAT/ACT—tests in which you'll never know what question is coming next.

Tackling the blocking problem

Think about the way you go through a typical school day. If you are like most students, your classes are scheduled in chunks. You might have one hour of biology, followed by an hour of math, followed by an hour-long class in world literature. If you are lucky, a gym class might break up your schedule. And within each class, chances are your teacher will introduce a single topic, explain the fundamentals, and then move on to the next topic. That pattern is called "blocked practice."

This type of schedule may make sense for a school administrator, but it is not a great way to learn. Instead of blocking, which entails reviewing a single topic at a time before moving on to the next subject, it turns out that interleaving, or mixing up the type of problems you study, is a more effective way to learn.

Say you are in geometry class and your teacher is explaining the Pythagorean theorem. Chances are she'll explain the topic and then give you a dozen practice problems on it. That's blocked practice in action, and although it might seem like an effective way to learn, it's not. Remember that on the SAT/ACT you aren't going to see twelve questions in a row that require the same solution. By simplifying her teaching method, the teacher has given you a crutch. The SAT/ACT is going to kick it away.

Now imagine an alternative way to study. This time your teacher explains the Pythagorean theorem, then gives you a set of problems not only related to that, but also other concepts drawn from all the math you've studied that year. What she is doing is called interleaving. At first it's going to seem a lot harder to remember all that math. But thanks to the retrieval effect we explained in Chapter Two, *Put Yourself to the Test,* it makes learning more effective. And it's a really powerful way to learn almost anything, from math, to art history, to hitting a curveball. But especially math.

Here's why interleaving is so effective

According to researchers, mixing things up reinforces the brain's ability to organize and differentiate between different kinds of problems and the methods needed to solve them.

For example, to solve an algebra problem, you have to first figure out the right method to solve it. Then you need to apply the method to get the answer.

Mixing up the problems helps you learn how to use a specific method to solve a problem and when to use it. By encountering different types of problems as you study, you get practice in discovering the correct solution method for each.

Another reason might be that because you are mixing up problems, the various solutions you try to apply are still fresh in your working memory. That encourages comparisons between the problems, which can help you find the right solution to the problems later.

By using practice sessions that mix up your study problems, you will be forced to choose the right strategy based on the problem itself. By juxtaposing different types of math problems to solve, you are forced to choose the right solution method first, then apply it to the problem to find the right answer, just like in a math SAT/ACT question.

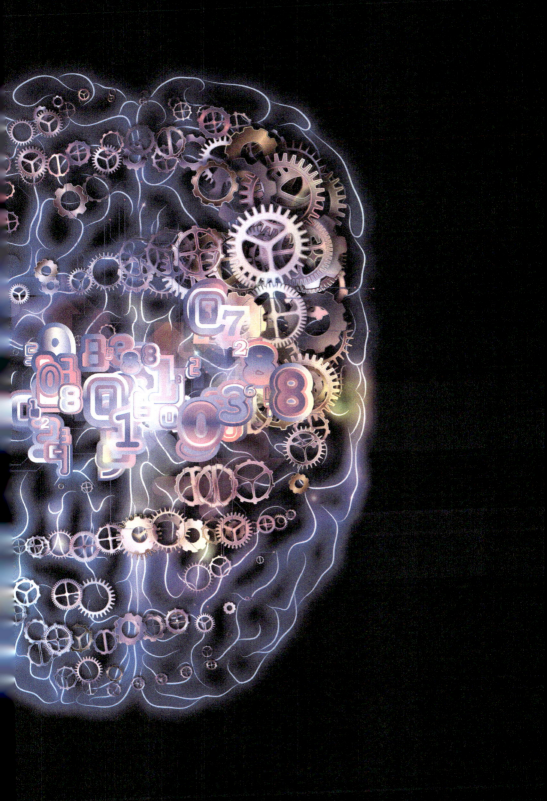

Why students love blocked practice, and why that's not a good thing

In blocked practice, you are given the correct strategy to use, followed by practice questions that require that you employ that strategy over and over again. That makes solving the practice problems a lot easier. Using the strategy over and over again creates a sense of "fluency," or familiarity, that results in you feeling confident you've mastered the problems. But that is the problem. The trouble is your sense of fluency masks the difference between short-term mastery and the long-term learning you'll need for the SAT/ACT.

When it comes to the SAT/ACT, you are given a problem, not the solution. The clue to finding the right strategy is included in the problem itself. By mixing up the problems you practice, you are building your ability to come up with different problem-solving strategies based on each new problem. And that's a much more effective way to prepare for the math questions on the SAT/ACT.

Blocked Approach   **Interleaved Approach**

Problem-solving strategies — Problem types   Problem-solving strategies — Problem types

65

Interleaving works

Psychologists who study learning techniques compared blocked practice with interleaved practice while teaching two groups of college students how to measure the volume of four different geometric solids. The first group read instructions on how to compute the volume of a specific solid and then practiced it four times in a row. Then they read another set of instructions for a different solid and had four more practice problems. They did this four times in a row, until they had solved all four solids. That's blocked practice.

The second group also worked on all four solids, but they mixed up the way they studied. First, they read all four sets of instructions. Then they worked through all the problems, but in a way that was different from the first group: every set of four problems included one problem from a different solid. That's interleaved practice. By mixing up—or interleaving—the problems, the students were forced to discriminate between the problems and learn the right formula to apply to each one.

One week after the instruction period, the students were tested. Those who were able to mix up the problems they studied using the interleaving technique scored more than three times higher than students who studied using the blocked practice method![2]

Solving new problems with old knowledge

Most of what we learn is based on what we already know. We build a body of knowledge based on what we have already observed to be true, which helps us learn new concepts and categories. Learning scientists call this "inductive learning."

To test whether interleaving or blocking would be better for our ability to solve new problems based on prior experience, researchers at UCLA asked students to study and learn the painting styles of 12 different painters. For half of the artists, all six of their paintings were shown one after another. For the other half of the artists, their paintings were mixed up with the paintings by other artists. During the final test, students were shown new paintings and asked to identify the artist who created each of them. In other words, they were using their old knowledge to solve a new problem.

When they were tested, 78 percent of the students got better results by mixing up the paintings from the different artists they studied. Interleaved practice was much better than blocked practice. But it gets even more interesting. When the same students were asked how effective the different study techniques were, 78 percent rated blocked practice as good as or better than interleaved practice—and this was after they had experienced the final test in which interleaving was more effective! In other words, students were poor judges of the effectiveness of their own study methods.[3] That means to adopt interleaving as an effective way to study, you'll have to overcome your preconceptions.

"I am always doing that which I cannot do, in order that I may learn how to do it."

— Pablo Picasso

TAKEAWAYS:

Begin with blocked practice.
When you take on a new topic or want to solve a new kind of problem, it's okay to start with a bit of blocked practice. This will help at first to familiarize your self with the subject.

Don't be fooled by fluency.
Blocked practice sessions deliver a false sense of mastery.

Mastery is in the mix.
By mixing up the topics you study, you build mental mastery.

Alternate problems, topics, and subjects.
Follow up blocked practice sessions with interleaving techniques to alternate the current problem with different types of problems you've learned in your previous study sessions.

Notes:

How will I mix up what I study to improve my learning?

5

HOW

WHEN

WHERE

STUDY

Keep It Fresh

For lasting learning, change up
where and how you study

Decades of research on learning and memory suggest that small changes in how we study, where we study, and when we study can make a big difference in how we learn. In this chapter, I will explain how keeping your study methods fresh can have a positive impact on improving your SAT/ACT scores.

Nobody likes change
except a baby with a wet diaper

From elementary school days, you've probably been told by your teachers to find a quiet place to study, and to do your homework in that same place at the same time, every time. Based on what learning scientists have discovered about effective study methods, it turns out there's a better way to study, and it contradicts pretty much everything we've been told about how we learn.

One of the most important findings coming from learning researchers involves changing the conditions of study. It's a topic they call "variability of practice" and basically it means that if we keep our practice methods fresh, continually mixing up the places, times, and conditions under which we study, we'll learn more. So instead of studying in the same place at the same time, you can actually improve your SAT/ACT scores if you change things up.

Here's how it works

Let's say you wanted to practice free throw shooting. You'd step up to the line, dribble the ball a couple of times, catch your breath, and shoot the ball at the back of the rim. And you'd do this over and over. That seems to make sense, since in the game, that's what happens. But it turns out a more effective way to practice shooting free throws is to take shots from different spots on the floor, from locations around the foul line. By mixing up the conditions of practice, you become even more familiar with the underlying skill you are trying to master. It's a bit harder at first, but it'll pay off in the end.

The findings are based on initial research by two learning researchers at the University of Ottawa. In their study, eight-year-old kids practiced throwing beanbags at a target on the floor. One group of kids varied the conditions of their practice by throwing the bean bags from distances of two feet and from four feet. The other group threw the beanbags from only three feet. Then both groups were tested on their ability to toss the beanbags from three feet.

If you had to predict which group of kids tossed most accurately, you would probably think that those who practiced from three feet would be better when tested from three feet. But that turned out to be wrong. The kids who mixed up their practice conditions and tossed the beanbags from two feet and four feet did better![1] The same results have been achieved when learning a forehand racket skill—like what you would see in tennis—and shooting a basketball.

What does that mean to you?

So changing how we practice shooting foul shots makes a difference in basketball. When it comes to studying for a test like the SAT/ACT, mixing up where and what you study can help you get better results, too.

You'll make more mistakes at first, but when it comes time to take the test, or learn a new skill, the different study conditions you've placed on yourself can actually boost your score.

Here's how it works

By studying in different places and mixing up the types of questions you study, you link your learning to a wider variety of memory cues. When it comes time to take the SAT/ACT, these cues can serve as triggers that can help you gain access to the answers you'll need.

To improve your scores, change where you study

In the late 1970s, researchers at the University of Michigan tried this out with university students who were asked to study lists of words in different places. Half the group studied 40 words in one room, and half the group studied the words in a different room. Three hours later, half of the students in each group returned to the same room to study the words again, whereas the other half restudied the words in the different room. So both groups studied the words twice, with the only difference being that half of the students studied both times in the same room and the other half studied in two different rooms. Three hours later, both groups were brought together in a neutral location—a room that none of the students had studied in—for a final test.

The researchers discovered something truly surprising. The students who studied in different rooms recalled nearly 25 of the words, whereas the students who studied in the same room recalled about 16 words. Just by changing the places where they studied, these students improved their scores.[2]

Mixing up where you study for the SAT/ACT doesn't just improve your verbal learning. It works with other subjects like math, too. Researchers conducted an experiment with students in statistics classes to learn if changing practice conditions would make a difference when it came to learning more difficult materials. Students who attended statistics classes held in four different locations over four different days scored better on tests than the students who attended all four lectures in the same room.[3]

Why it matters

When you take a test like the SAT/ACT, chances are good you'll be taking it at an unfamiliar location and at an unfamiliar time. By changing the places you study, you can improve your test score. At the same time, you'll reduce your anxiety about taking it in a new place.

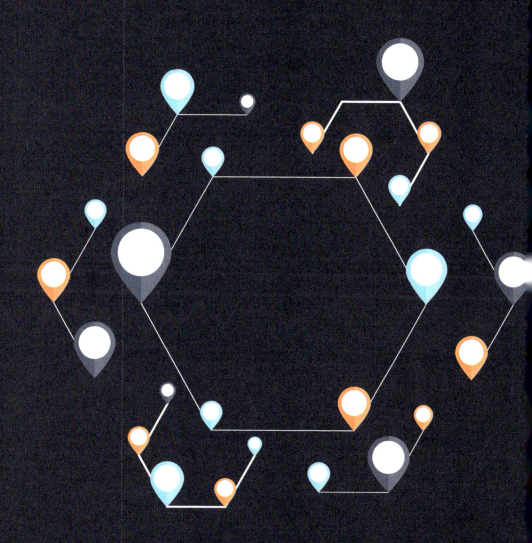

The difference makes the difference

So changing the place where you study can make a difference. Changing the types of problems you study can make a positive difference, too.

Researchers wanted to find out if solving multiple versions of anagrams would make a difference when it came to learning. One group of participants got the same anagrams to solve three separate times during a study period. For example, they tried to solve the anagram LDOOF three times. Another group had to solve multiple versions of the same word. This group had to practice on DOLOF, FOLOD, and OOFLD. But only LDOOF appeared on the final test. When it came to the final test, the group that practiced on a variety of problems scored better.[4]

In other words, even though the second group had never seen the anagram LDOOF before, they still solved it more often than the group that had practiced it three times. That goes against much of what we think about how to study. But it shows that by increasing the variation in the types of problems we study, we can broaden the base of our knowledge, and potentially score higher when it comes to taking the SAT/ACT.

LDOOF DOLOF

LDOOF FOLOD

LDOOF OOFLD

LDOOF LDOOF

"We now accept the fact that learning is a lifelong process of keeping abreast of change. And the most pressing task is to teach people how to learn."

— Peter Drucker

TAKEAWAYS:

To master the SAT/ACT, mix up where you study.
Instead of going to your favorite spot in the library to study, mix it up. Find new places to study. Empty classrooms, the cafeteria, study hall, your kitchen table. Try studying standing up. Changing the conditions of study can potentially help you score higher on the SAT/ACT.

Vary your practice problems.
By mixing up the types of problems you study, you'll force your brain to work harder to solve them. Instead of an automatic response to problem solving, your brain is forced to make the effort to distinguish the similarities and differences as you work to find a solution to each new problem.

Distinctions make the difference.
Because you have made your learning more distinctive, you'll have made it more memorable, and that means you'll be able to transfer what you've learned more easily to the SAT/ACT exam room.

Put the practice in "variable practice."
Sign up for a SAT/ACT practice test that gives you new problems to solve every day.

Notes:

How will I change my study conditions
to keep my learning fresh?

Explain Yourself

Why learning to ask "why?" and "how?" matters

To learn something, explain it. That's an idea behind active learning. It's a learning approach that encourages students to ask "why?" and "how?" and to come up with their own examples while studying.

Remember your third grade book report on worms? Whatever your topic, chances are good you *do* remember it, because you had to stand in front of your class and tell them the whole slimy story. By talking about what you know in your own words, you make your learning memorable. You may not remember anyone else's book report, but when your teacher asked you to stand and deliver, she made your learning active. Active learning demands you explain yourself and elaborate on what you know. It's an easy-to-learn technique you can build into your study habits. Even better, it really works.

How well does it work?

Undergraduates who participated in an active learning study at a Canadian university scored a 72 percent on a recall test compared to the 37 percent scored by their peers.

Researchers gave students in three groups a number of sentences to study, such as "The hungry man got into the car." The active learners were asked to provide an explanation. In other words, they had to come up with their own answer to "why?" The other students either were given an explanation or didn't receive one at all.

By prompting students to come up with their own explanation for a fact, they had to generate an answer, which boosted their learning.[1] Learning scientists believe the process requires the brain to integrate new information with what it already knows and then discriminate between facts to find one that is true. And as study after study shows, when you come up the answers yourself, you learn even more effectively.

Word up!

When studying vocabulary definitions for the SAT/ACT, it is helpful to use the word in context by generating your own sentence using the new word. If you're already given a sentence with the word in it, try coming up with a different sentence on your own.

Here's how it works

Hang out with a four-year-old and you soon discover their favorite word is "why?". They want an explanation for the world around them. It turns out that the action of explaining a topic, a concept, a definition, or a math problem—in your own words—forces you to integrate what you've just learned with what you already know. In the process, you make your leaning more durable and strengthen your ability to recall what you know on the SAT/ACT.

**The more you know,
the more you learn**

One of the interesting side effects discovered by researchers who study active learning is that the more you already know, the more your scores will rise. Your prior knowledge of a subject acts like a booster rocket for your brain, amplifying the impact of active learning.

To test that theory, researchers gave students in Canada and Germany a list of facts about Canada and Germany. When the students were tested using the active learning technique on how well they could recall these facts, the German students scored high on the new materials about Germany. And the Canadian kids scored high on the new material about Canada.

But when they switched the test, asking German kids about the Canadian facts and Canadian students about the German facts, their scores plummeted. The difference was profound.

Students who already had a background of expertise scored twice as high over those who did not. The researchers discovered that if you already have a foundation of knowledge—what psychologists call "domain expertise"—you will benefit even more when you ask yourself to answer your own questions.[2]

In other words, the more you already know, the better you will learn.

Active learning works

Psychologists have tried this technique in labs with small groups of students who were asked to read facts about animals, the reasons for the dinosaur extinction, and accounting principles. Each time, the results showed that participants achieved higher scores when they used the active learning technique of asking themselves "why is this true?" and then came up with a factual answer.

Researchers have discovered that active learning techniques are incredibly effective in the classroom, too. In a university biology class, students had to learn a long section on human digestion. Half of the students were given 21 separate prompts interspersed about every 150 words, as a reminder to ask themselves "why is this true?". The other students simply studied at their own pace, like normal, without any prompts.

In the follow-up test, the students prompted to ask themselves "why is this true?" scored five points higher. What's more, it didn't take them much longer to read the material using the active learning technique. Students who stopped to ask themselves "why?" took 32 minutes to get through the material compared to the 28 minutes for students who simply read straight through the section.[3]

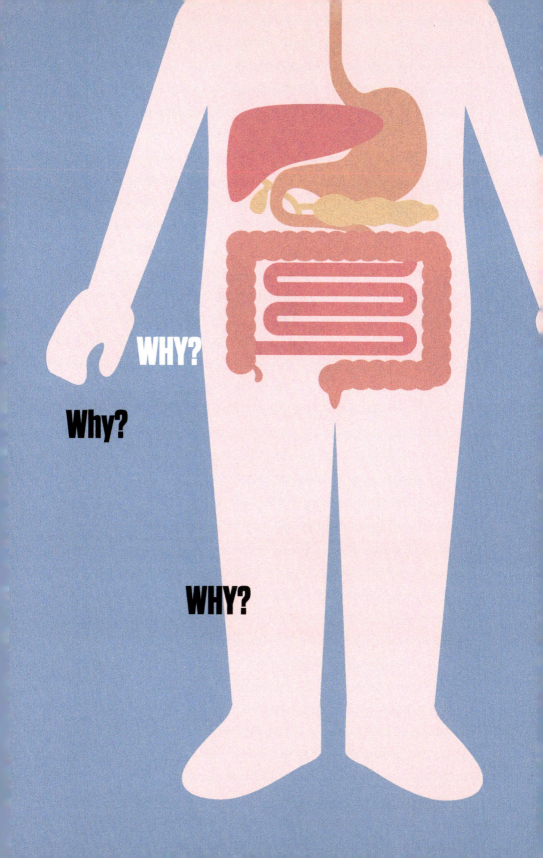

From why to how:
explaining the process of
how you learn and why it matters

Okay, you've learned to ask yourself why something is true. Researchers have discovered an additional technique that also reinforces learning. They call it "self-explanation," and it means explaining to yourself the basic method of how you learned some new fact or solved a problem. In other words, instead of explaining a concept, you explain your thinking.

In 1983, Diane Berry, a psychologist who studies how we learn, gave students a series of logical reasoning puzzles. Berry explained how to do the puzzles and then let students try to solve the puzzles for themselves. One group was asked to think out loud and explain the techniques they used to solve the puzzles. After an initial trial, most students could solve the puzzles correctly. Next, Berry asked her students to move on to more abstract problems.

The students who used the active learning technique of self-explanation were able to solve the abstract problems much more accurately. Simply by explaining to themselves how they were able to solve one set of problems, students built a foundation for solving more difficult ones.[4]

The effect of self-explanation works across a body of knowledge, helping to reinforce what you've learned across different tasks and within different domains. Researchers have shown self-explanation works with logic puzzles, math problems in elementary school, and algebra formulas and geometry theorems for high school students. You'll also be glad to know that self-explanation has proven effective on tests that require fill-in-the-blank and multiple choice tests— just like the SAT/ACT.

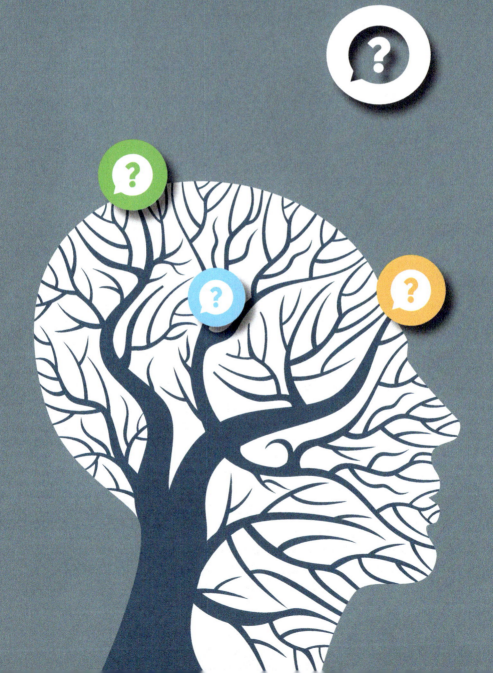

How it works

Day in, day out, teachers encourage you to learn new facts, expand the boundaries of what you know, and master new domains of knowledge. As you take in all that information, stop for a moment and explain the process of how you are learning to yourself. This "self-explanation" helps your brain integrate the new material with what you already know. And it's this active integration of knowledge that helps it stick.

Asking yourself "why?" and "how?" is a great learning technique you can use for the rest of your life, not just as you prepare for the SAT/ACT. Society demands we all become lifelong learners, but that doesn't mean we're going to go through life with highlighters in our hands. Having a reliable, proven, easy-to-use technique that helps us learn anything is a huge advantage. You'll use it in college and graduate school. You can apply it at work. It can even help you master new hobbies, games, and activities.

"A wise man can learn more from a foolish question than a fool can learn from a wise answer"

— Bruce Lee

TAKEAWAYS:

Build explanation and elaboration into your study habits.
Explain a concept in your own words to yourself and try to come up with your own examples to support the concept.

As you study, ask yourself "why is this true?".
Coming up with the answer can potentially help raise your SAT/ACT score.

Keep it simple.
When it comes to learning facts, a straightforward approach is best. Why did the hungry man get into the car? To go to the restaurant.

More is better.
Instead of asking yourself "why?" every couple of pages as you study, use the active learning technique more frequently, after a paragraph or two.

Learning is a process.
By explaining to yourself how you learn, you move from simple memorization of facts to an active procedure for learning new information.

The harder the material, the better it works.
When you are really struggling with the material, stop and try to explain it to yourself. Ask yourself why it matters and then come up with your own answer.

Notes:

How will I build the concepts of explanation and elaboration into my study habits?

Teach It to Learn It

To raise your score, don't just study a subject, teach it

That's the advice of researchers who study the benefits of tutoring. As you might expect, tutoring helps the tutored students learn: the student sees their scores go up and their grades rise. But tutoring also helps the tutors learn! Not only do they learn more, their attitude toward the subject can improve, and so can their self-confidence. Researchers call it the "tutor learning effect." I call it win-win.

One group of researchers took a look at 38 different studies that examined the effects of tutoring on learning. In 33 of the studies they reported, tutoring was shown to boost learning in the tutors themselves.[1] It didn't matter what subject they were teaching, either. Reading, math, psychology, history, biology—across the board, the people who served as tutors saw their scores rise. What's more, the tutors' attitudes toward the subject matter improved and so did their self-concept. So if you hate algebra, you might learn to love it—if you teach it.

Turbocharge your tutoring

You can boost your learning through teaching even more if you add this simple technique: build in question-and-answer sessions. By responding to questions that people ask, you force yourself to retrieve the information from long-term memory and explain the material in your own words. Retrieval practice is a very powerful way to enhance learning. You can learn more about it in Chapter Two, *Put Yourself to the Test.*

Researchers who studied this effect discovered that middle school students who were prompted to answer questions about the material they were teaching learned more effectively thanks to the students integrating ideas on their own to explain the principle-based concepts.[2]

Some of these questions you get asked might arise out of confusion, lack of understanding, or simply because the material presented was wrong. And that's good. Here's why: when a student asks a question that reveals a hole in your own knowledge, it forces you to take another look at what you know (or, in this case, what you *don't* know).

"You do not really understand something unless you can explain it to your grandmother."

— Albert Einstein

In other words, questions, wrong answers, and confusion can help you identify gaps in your knowledge. If you are having a hard time explaining something to someone, it's usually a pretty good clue you don't understand the topic all that well. If it turns out that you are the source of the error, you have to fix it. How? By relearning it. Try the "interleaving" learning strategy outlined in Chapter Four, *Mix It Up*, or spacing out your study sessions as we recommended in Chapter Three, *Space It Out*. No matter what topic you take on, be sure to adopt a growth mindset as explained in Chapter One, so you can see your challenges as opportunities to succeed.

Go deep

Good questions demand great answers, and great answers build learning. Researchers have discovered that questions requiring logical reasoning, detailed explanations, and the ability to connect two different ideas create stronger learning compared to shallow questions that just ask for facts.

Examples of this can include deep questions such as "how does that work?" and "why does this matter?". By coming up with answers to these questions, you force yourself to forge new connections and find new examples that strengthen your understanding and learning. Take a look at Chapter 6, *Explain Yourself,* to learn more about the learning benefits of asking "how?" and "why?".

Weird science

Simply by *expecting* to teach a subject, learning improves. It sounds crazy, but it works.

Learning scientists who wanted to study the effect teaching has on learning came up with an interesting experiment. They took 56 UCLA undergraduate students, split them into two groups, and asked both groups to study the same passage about the Crimean War. One group was told they would be tested on it. The other group was told they wouldn't be tested, but instead that they would have to teach the material to another student who would be tested.

At the end of the study session, the researchers did something a little tricky. They told the group of "teachers" that the student they were supposed to teach got sick. So they were off the hook. Instead, the researchers tested both groups on the passage. The students who expected to teach scored higher.

During a free recall test, the students who were told they were going to have to explain the material to a peer produced more complete and better-organized answers. In other words, students expecting to teach learned more than the students who were told they would be tested.[3]

Expecting to teach is an effective, simple learning technique, and it's one that you can take advantage of while you are preparing for the SAT/ACT. Every once in a while, think to yourself "how would I explain this to someone else?".

Prepare to teach

As we go through school, we are expected to learn a number of subjects. Many students set their goal to learn the material, get the highest grade possible, check the box, and move on.

But what if we set a higher goal? What if, before we started studying, we adopted the goal of teaching the material, not just studying it? According to psychologists who study how we learn, students who changed their expectation—from expecting a test to expecting to teach—changed their ability to learn new material.

It's a finding that surprised even the psychologists who studied it. They expected the university students who served as their participants would have plenty of experience taking tests. Teaching a subject, on the other hand, would be unfamiliar and could produce anxiety around public speaking. For these reasons, researchers predicted expecting to teach would have a negative effect on the students' learning, yet it turned out to be better than expecting a test.[3]

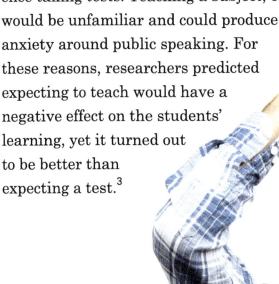

Here's how it works

When you expect to teach a subject, you bring into play the critical activities that build learning. Before you can explain a topic to someone else, you have to engage with it. This means you summarize the material, identify the main points you want to get across, and mentally organize the information in your mind. Then you can communicate it in a way that will make sense. It's a process of engagement that includes explanations, analogies, and finding examples. As you teach, you actively explain the materials, answer questions, and correct errors.

With each of these activities, you naturally create the opportunity to rehearse what you know about the material. As you are learning new material and generating new ideas, you'll also uncover gaps in your knowledge and discover misconceptions. As you correct errors, you are building knowledge.

All of these activities are powerful learning strategies that help you encode the material so you can remember it when it comes time to take the SAT/ACT.

Just for parents

To improve your student's SAT/ACT scores, here's a quick, (almost) painless way to do it. Ask them to teach you the topic they are studying.

Before they crack open a book or hit the Internet to study a topic, ask them to be ready to explain it to you when they finish. Taking a few minutes to explain a new subject of study is a great way to drive their learning home and reinforce their memory. As an added bonus, you might learn something, too.

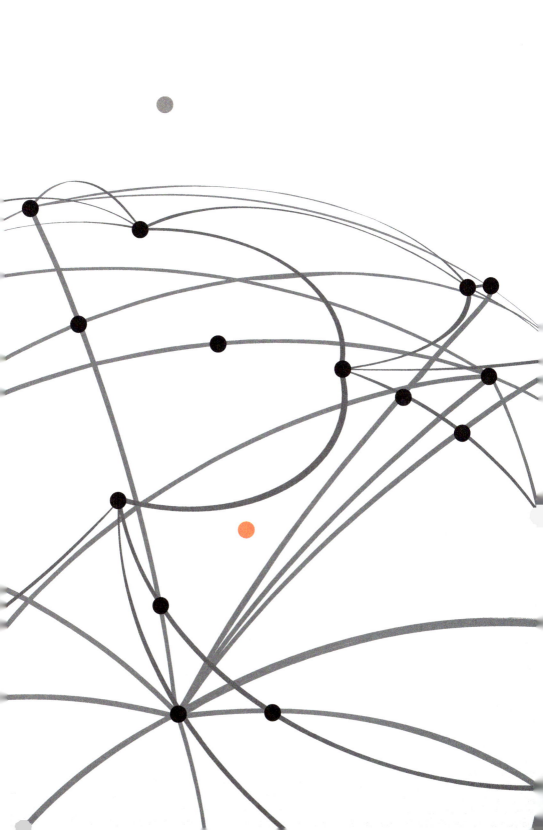

"In learning you will teach, and in teaching you will learn."

— Phil Collins

TAKEAWAYS:

If you want to learn something, teach it.
Find a study partner you can tutor. She'll learn something, but so will you.

Explain, elaborate, extrapolate.
Forcing yourself to explain what you have learned helps you build stronger memories of that material.

Know what you don't know.
Teaching someone else reveals gaps in your own knowledge, and that's good, because it tells you which topics need to be relearned.

Build in Q&A.
Include opportunities for questions and answers when you teach someone. Answering questions—especially *how* and *why* questions that demand more elaborate answers—stimulates the learning process.

Study it like you are going to teach it.
Study your subjects as if you were about to explain the concept to someone else. Even if you only *expect* to teach, you'll remember more and potentially score higher on the SAT/ACT.

Notes:

How will I use teaching as a learning strategy and who can I teach?

Look Back to Move Forward

How to raise your scores through self-reflection

It sounds simple, but learning researchers have discovered reflection is a powerful technique to boost your learning, your memory, and even your self-confidence. No, it doesn't mean taking a look at yourself in the mirror. It means looking back at your day, thinking about what you learned, and spending 15 minutes jotting down your thoughts about what you have studied. It can help you raise your scores on your SAT/ACT, and as you head into the work force in later years, it's been shown to raise performance at work, too.

How to do it

Keep a notebook, or use your laptop or tablet if you have one. At the end of the day, take the time to reflect back on the lectures you attended and the material you studied. Write down the key points your teacher made. Ask yourself how the new information you learned connects to what you've already got under your belt. Build on the concepts of what you learned by coming up with new examples.

If you are covering new material or working on new skills, make a list of the good, the bad, and the ugly. List your successes, take note of where you fell short, and write down what you could work on next time to do better.

Remember to use your own words and ideas, and don't just copy the notes you took in class. By writing down your own ideas about what you've learned, you are engaging in two powerful learning strategies educators call "retrieval" and "elaboration." By generating your own summary of what you learned that day, you make your brain work in precisely the right ways to build even more learning. You can learn more about these techniques in Chapter Two, *Put Yourself to the Test,* and Chapter Six, *Explain Yourself.*

How it works

15-minute journaling sessions are great examples of stimulus and response. Your study sessions introduce the stimulus, reflection ensures your brain organizes the stimulus as new learning, and then you respond by improving your memory.

To get better results, study less

Say you have blocked out a few hours to study. Instead of using the full time period to hit the books, set aside the last 15 minutes for reflection. Write down what went well, what you think you learned, and where you think you can do better. That's all it takes.

Judge your own learning

To make rapid improvements in your learning, judge it yourself. Instead of waiting for your report card, take a moment to judge how well you are doing, right *now*. According to researchers who have studied the phenomenon, the process of judging how well you are learning can itself boost learning.

My colleagues at UCLA and I tested whether the act of judging one's memory changes one's memory. We had 40 students attempt to learn pairs of words that were strongly related to each other—for example, *pledge-promise* and *blunt-sharp*. One group of students was asked to judge their own performance by estimating their ability to successfully recall each word pair on a future test. In other words, they attempted to forecast their own learning. The other group of students was not asked to predict their learning. Instead, they studied the words uninterrupted.

When both groups were tested on their ability to remember the word pairs later, it turned out that the group of students who were asked to make judgments about how well they were learning scored higher. In fact, they were able to recall nearly 70 percent of the word pairs, whereas the students who did not judge their learning recalled about 50 percent of the word pairs. We think that making judgments about your learning may strengthen the connections that link the material you are studying. Judging your learning, it turns out, can enhance your learning.[1]

Here's how it works

When students are asked to evaluate their own learning—how well they did in class, what they want to study next, how long they want to study it, and what they might want to restudy—they usually focus on the most difficult material or the areas where they are weakest. And that primes the brain to accelerate new learning.

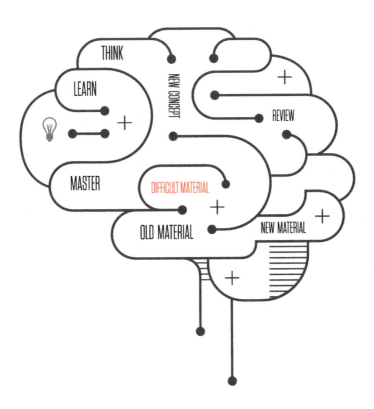

Sleep on it

Can you get smarter in your sleep? The answer is yes! Okay, there's a slight catch. You have to prepare yourself mentally before lights out. Taking those 15 minutes of reflection just before you go to sleep will help you remember more and remember better when you wake up. You can also use the technique of studying just before sleep to improve your ability to recall new information.

Researchers at Harvard tried this out with 207 students. The students were given word pairs to study. One group of students studied the words at 9 o'clock in the morning. The other group studied the word pairs at 9 o'clock at night. The scientists discovered that those students who were able to study the words just before they went to sleep had significantly better recall the next day compared to those who studied the information in the morning.[2]

Why it works

Scientists believe that studying just before sleep helps the brain consolidate, or stabilize, the memory of newly-learned information. That means remembering will be stronger when you wake up. It also prevents forgetting by slowing down the impact of new events as they erase the old.

**"It is what
we know already
that often prevents
us from learning."**

— Claude Bernard

TAKEAWAYS:

Get a journal and use it.

At the end of the day, spend 15 minutes writing down what you learned from your SAT/ACT study sessions.

Don't copy your notes.

Use your own words to write down what you learned. Retrieving information from long-term memory will boost your learning and improve your scores.

Make a list.

Your personal evaluation of the material you've mastered, along with the areas where you need improvement, will help you become a more efficient learner.

Make your own judgments.

Reflect on your own learning while you are studying. As strange as it may sound, the process of evaluating your own learning can strengthen learning.

Sleep is your friend.

Instead of staying up all night studying for the SAT/ACT, be sure you get a good amount of rest every night, and try to study a bit before you doze off. Studying just before you sleep can enhance learning by stabilizing your memories.

Notes:

How will I use self-reflection to improve my learning?

Imagine That

*Ancient memory techniques you
can use today to raise your scores*

No one expects you to memorize all the answers on the
SAT/ACT, but you can strengthen your memory using a
few easy-to-use mental techniques. Use these strategies
while you study and you can reinforce your learning by
building stronger, more durable memories. One thing to
remember when it comes to memory, however: it is important that you actually take the time to understand the
material you are learning. Once you understand what you
are studying, these techniques will make it easier to recall
what you know.

Mental gymnastics

There are tried-and-true memory-building techniques that date back to the ancient Greeks. They are still in use today, especially in Memory Championships, competitions in which mental athletes test their powers of recall against challenges that require them to memorize hundreds of words, decks of cards, strings of digits, and more.

The feats of mental ability are astounding. In 2015, at the USA Memory Championships, Lance Tschirhart recalled 52 cards in 29 seconds. In 2011, Sophia Hu reeled off 120 words in a row before a miss.

These mental gymnasts achieve their extraordinary results using tricks popularized by Greek scholars thousands of years ago. They are called mnemonics (pronounced "neh-mahniks" – the first "m" is silent) after Mnemosyne, the Greek goddess of memory.

Our story begins with a gruesome disaster. In the 5th century BC, a poet was asked to give a recital at a banquet hall. Midway through, he stepped outside to greet some late arrivals. At that precise moment, an earthquake struck. The building collapsed, killing everyone inside. Not only that, the bodies were so mangled they were unrecognizable, even to their own families. The only survivor was that poet. Amazingly, he was able to recall the names of everyone there.

He did it with the aid of a simple memory trick: he remembered where everyone was sitting. Based on the mental picture of the locations where people sat, he was able to recall all their names.

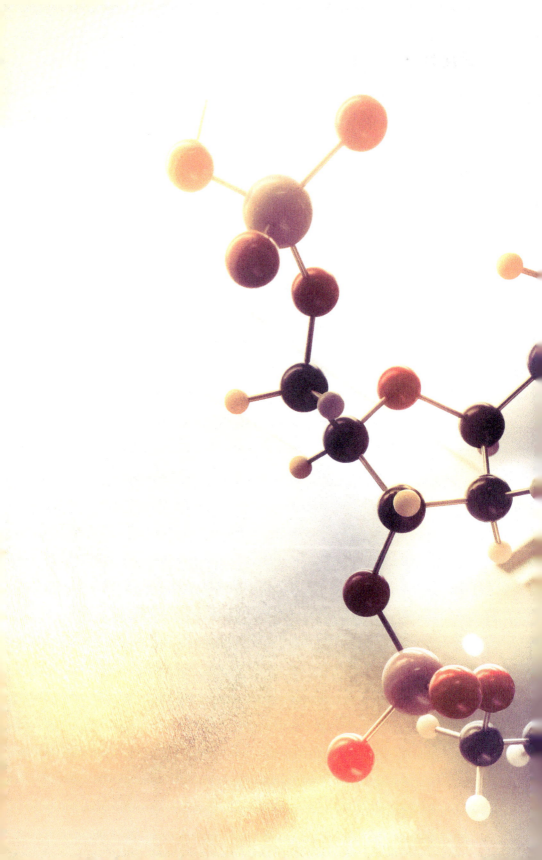

Picture this

You can build your own mental imagery as you study, and you don't have to wait for the roof to fall in, either. As you read through the material you want to study, simply assign a clear mental image to each paragraph of new material.

This act of linking mental pictures to textbook study was the subject of research by three university learning scientists. In 2009, they gave 10th graders 35 minutes to study a complicated science text that explained the characteristics of water molecules. One group of students was asked to study the material by reading for comprehension, just like they would normally do. The other group was told to read the material and mentally imagine the content one paragraph at a time by creating a simple, clear picture in their minds.

When they were tested a short time later, the group that built mental images scored much higher on their exam. Scientists believe these students achieved better results because the act of creating imagery enhances the brain's ability to organize information. By linking distinctive visual images to information in the text, the students created their own coherent story—a mental exercise that reinforced their understanding of the material.[1]

There's a reason for the saying "a picture is worth a thousand words." Pictures are easy to remember. Words, not so much.

Mental floss

Here are a few techniques you can use to help you remember the material you study.

Acronyms

Of all the tricks you can use to reinforce your memory, one of the simplest is acronyms. These are combinations of the first letters of words that together spell out a new word. You may know some of these already, such as ROY G BIV, which is an acronym for the visible colors of the spectrum, or HOMES, which spells out the first letters of the Great Lakes. You can create your own acronyms, too. Simply build a list of the words you want to remember and then use the first letters of each word to form a new, easy-to-remember word.

4COL	AYOR	DDG	FOC	IJS	OAO
1daful	B&F	DFWLY	FSR	IME	OBTW
GR8	BBFN	DHYB	FYC	IMS	OTL
2G2BT	BBIAS	DJM	G2G	JAD	PIR
AAR	BCNU	DNBL8	G98T	KMP	PMJI
ACK	BFN	DTRT	GFN	LBH	RGR
ADBB	BKA	DYFM	GMTA	LOL	ROTFL
AFAGAY	BYKI	E2HO	gratz	LMAO	RUT
AFASIC	CIL	EM	H2CUS	LTNS	SIT
AML	COS	EOM	HBTU	MIRL	STS
AOYP	CUNS	F2T	IBRB	NAGI	TFX
ASAYGT	D8	FFA	IBTD	NIH	TTTT

Acrostics

Acrostics are great ways to remember the order of items in a list. Think of these as acronyms in reverse. Instead of coming up with the first letters of each word, you begin with a list and then use the first letters of the items to create a new phrase. Examples of this technique include ways to remember the order of planets, as in My Very Educated Mom Just Served Us Nine Peanuts (Mercury, Venus, Earth, Mars, Jupiter, Saturn, Uranus, Neptune, Pluto), or the order of taxonomy in biology: Keep Pots Clean Or Family Gets Sick (kingdom, phylum, class, order, family, genus, species).

My **V**ery **E**ducated **M**om **J**ust **S**erved **U**s **N**ine **P**eanuts.

Rhymes and songs

The English alphabet is an abstract system of 26 letters. What kind of Einstein can remember all 26 components? And yet we manage to teach it to four-year-olds. How do we do it? With a song set to the tune of "Twinkle, Twinkle, Little Star."

If you've ever had to memorize poetry, you've probably discovered poems that rhyme are easier to recite from memory than free verse. Here's a rhyme you may have learned in your second grade session on history: "in fourteen-hundred-ninety-two, Columbus sailed the ocean blue." Of course, there's a rhyme to help you remember some of your spelling lessons as well: "I before E, except after C."

Memory palace

To remember more complex material, many mental gymnasts use a technique called the "method of loci," which essentially means assigning items to a specific place. They build a memory palace, or large mental mansion, and place the visual images of items they want to remember in each room. That's the memory technique our 5th century poet used to remember people's names after the earthquake.

For example, think about your drive to school. To use the method of loci, you associate the visual signposts along the way with specific things you want to remember. By linking these vivid mental images to a specific, real, and easy-to-remember place, you make them more memorable. When it comes time to take a test, you simply send your mind on the drive to school and use the landmarks along this mental path to help you recall the material.

"Education is learning what you didn't even know you didn't know."

— Daniel Boorstin

TAKEAWAYS:

The imagery-friendly SAT/ACT.

Imagery techniques are probably best suited for the critical reading section of the SAT/ACT because the reading section is more imagery-friendly than, say, math problems.

Every picture tells a story.

Pictures are easier to remember than words. When you encounter a critical reading passage, such as a narrative or short story, generating your own mental imagery can reinforce what you are reading and help embed it in your memory.

A system for sequence.

When you encounter material in which the order of things is important—say, the order of the US Presidents or the dates the 13 colonies entered the union—you can use memory techniques like acrostics or the method of loci to help you remember them.

Notes:

What memory mnemonics will I
incorporate into my study sessions?

Visualize Your Path to Success

Practical visualization techniques you can use to achieve your learning goals

In one of the most famous visualization experiments ever conducted, college students were asked to shoot 100 free throws. One group practiced shooting free throws for 20 minutes a day, five days a week. A second group did nothing. And a third group visualized shooting free throws. No basketball, no basket, no rim, no net. Just their minds. Four weeks later, the students were asked to take 100 shots at the basket. The first group improved 24 percent. The second group made no improvement. The third group, the ones that painted a picture in their mind without ever touching a basketball, scored 23 percent higher. Simply by mentally rehearsing the steps to shoot a free throw, they improved almost as much as the group that actually practiced with a real ball and goal.[1]

It seems that just by visualizing successful performance, you can improve your results.

I'm not suggesting you visualize a perfect score on the SAT/ACT and call it quits. Instead of fantasizing about your success, I'd like to recommend a more effective visualization technique to help you score better on the SAT/ACT.

It's all about process. Instead of visualizing the results, you visualize the steps required to reach your goal. According to psychologists who study the mechanics of how we learn, merely thinking through the separate steps required to reach a future goal (instead of the outcome) can improve your study, increase your ability to plan, decrease your anxiety, and improve your grades.

In 1999, two researchers at UCLA wanted to see for themselves whether visualizing the process or the outcome made a difference in students' performance. They gave a group of 100 college freshmen an assignment. A week before their midterm exam, they asked one group to think about all the steps they would need to perform in order to study well for their midterm. These students were instructed to visualize where, when, and how they might study in order to get a high grade on an exam. They visualized the process.

Meanwhile, they asked a second group of students to visualize getting a good grade on the same exam. These students were instructed to see themselves finishing the exam, getting a great grade, and imagining how they would feel. In other words, this group visualized the outcome.

The exam grades revealed some pretty interesting results. When their grades were handed out following the midterm, the students who visualized the process of achieving a higher grade did exactly that. They outscored the outcome-oriented students by more than eight percentage points. That's enough to make a whole letter grade difference.

Visualizing the process improved students' planning and reduced their anxiety, which ultimately led to more effective studying and better grades. On the other hand, visualizing the outcome reduced students' motivation and led them to overestimate the amount of time they would actually devote to studying.[2]

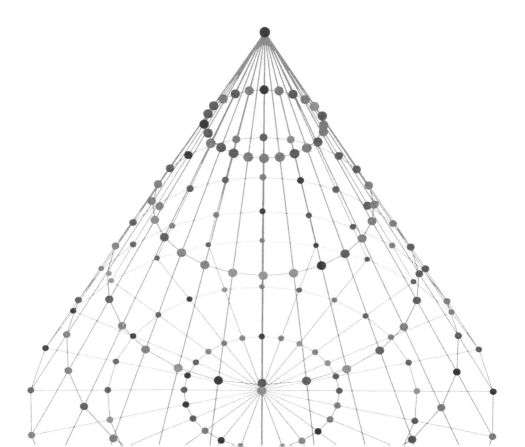

Here's how it works

When you visualize the process needed to achieve a goal, your brain strengthens the links between thought and action. Having a detailed mental picture helps build the real-world path required to reach a goal. Focusing on the process supports problem-solving—in this case, leading students to increase the amount of hours they studied—and at the same time it removes limitations to study, like anxiety. And that leads to better grades.

The law of the five Ps: Prior Planning Prevents Poor Performance
The UCLA psychologists asked themselves why the process-oriented group did better than the outcome-oriented group. They came up with an answer related to the "planning fallacy." Basically, the planning fallacy means that when people plan for an outcome instead of the process, they assume everything will work out just as they planned. They become overly optimistic about the amount of time needed to complete a task, leading them to underestimate the time needed, and often fail to anticipate problems that are likely to occur along the way. On the other hand, people who think through the process are able to anticipate potential problems and plan for them accordingly. In a nutshell, visualizing the path to success can protect you against the planning fallacy.

Turn thought into action

To reach your goals, visualize them. This is a variation on the old adage "if you don't know where you are going, you'll never get there." So take a moment to get goal-directed. Give yourself a few minutes of quiet time and rehearse in your mind the future events you'll likely encounter during the SAT/ACT. Write down your goals. By making this vision of the future as explicit as possible, you enhance your ability to construct a pathway to actually getting there. Then put your plan into action.

Start by visualizing yourself getting a great score on the SAT/ACT. Be specific when you set a goal for the SAT/ACT math and verbal. A 720? 750? 800? Go for it. Now, mentally build a picture in your mind of everything you need to do to achieve that great score.

Success is just a step away
When you mentally rehearse the steps required for successfully attaining your goal, you bring it into focus. By making the goal seem attainable, you build your self-confidence, and this can motivate you to try harder. And that can lead to better results when it comes time to take the SAT/ACT.

Keep that goal in your mind as you visualize the process of how to achieve it. Close your eyes and take it step by step. Imagine the specific steps you plan to take to do well on the SAT/ACT. Will you need a tutor? Do you plan on studying with a group of friends? Visualize how often you will meet, where you will study, and how much time you plan on studying. Remember, cramming for the SAT/ACT is counterproductive. Take a look at Chapter Three, *Space It Out,* for advice on how to schedule your study periods for best results.

Now take a moment to write down the steps you just visualized, including your motivation to do well, the level of effort you plan to put into studying, and the confidence you feel about the results you will achieve.

It is powerful technique that has been shown to raise test scores. Best of all, it doesn't take long. Those high-scoring UCLA students were able to raise their scores using visualization techniques that took them only five minutes a day.

Visualize less stress

There may be nothing more stressful in your life right now than taking the SAT/ACT. That's understandable because there's a lot riding on the outcome. You can harness the stress you feel to take action, or you can let it stand in your way.

Here's where visualization techniques are your friend:

Visualization builds confidence.
By actively imagining the events that will occur in the future, you naturally become more confident that these events will occur. By simulating the likelihood of an event, you prime yourself to take action.

Visualization promotes planning.
Simply by imagining the sequence of events that is about to happen helps you plan for it. It's an essential step to building an effective action plan.

Visualization feels good.
Mental simulation harnesses the right emotions and helps reduce the negative ones that prevent you from taking action. By mentally planning ahead, you get the benefit of reducing the anxiety around the future event, and you psych yourself up to take action.

"Failure is instuctive. The person who really thinks learns quite as much from his failures as from his successes."

— John Dewey

TAKEAWAYS:

Visualize the process, not outcomes.
Instead of thinking to yourself "I can do it!", you can get better results by thinking "here's *how* I can do it."

Keep it real.
By mentally rehearsing a real, practical plan of action to achieve your goals, you actually prompt yourself to take action. Think about how and when the other strategies outlined in this book can be used to achieve your learning goals.

Eliminate roadblocks.
Visualizing the process of success can help you overcome the negative emotions that prevent you from taking action, like anxiety and fear of failure.

Build a pathway.
Visualizing the steps required to achieve your goal reveals the path you need to take. By thinking through each step you need to take, you bring your goal into focus and make it that much closer to reality.

Stop worrying, start planning.
Visualizing the steps required to achieve your goal will reduce your anxiety. By planning more, you will worry less.

Five minutes a day.
It doesn't take long to visualize the steps to success. By practicing visualization techniques for five minutes a day, you'll take one of the essential steps toward achieving your goal: a great score on the SAT/ACT.

Notes:

How will I visualize my path to success?

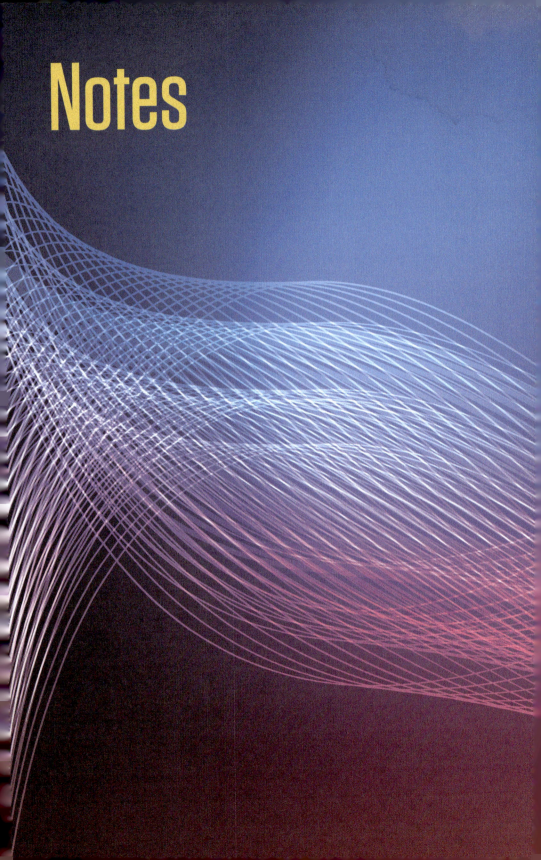

Foreword: The Increasing Importance of Knowing How to Learn

[1] Bjork, E. L., & Bjork, R. A. (2014). Making things hard on yourself, but in a good way: Creating desirable difficulties to enhance learning. In M. A. Gernsbacher and J. Pomerantz (Eds.), *Psychology and the real world: Essays illustrating fundamental contributions to society (2nd edition)* (pp. 59-68). New York, NY: Worth Publishers.

[2] Bjork, R.A. (1994). Memory and metamemory considerations in the training of human beings. In J. Metcalfe and A. Shimamura (Eds.), *Metacognition: Knowing about knowing* (pp.185-205). Cambridge, MA: MIT Press.

[3] Bjork, R. A., & Linn, M. C. (2002). Introducing desirable difficulties for educational applications in science (IDDEAS). *Cognition and Student Learning Grant R305H020113, Institute for Educational Sciences.*

[4] Dweck, C. S. (2006). *Mindset: The New Psychology of Success.* New York, NY: Random House.

Introduction: Learning Doesn't Work the Way You Think It Does

[1] Bjork, R. A. (1994). Memory and metamemory considerations in the training of human beings. In J. Metcalfe and A. Shimamura (Eds.), *Metacognition: Knowing about knowing* (pp.185-205). Cambridge, MA: MIT Press.
See also:
Bjork, E. L., & Bjork, R. A. (2014). Making things hard on yourself, but in a good way: Creating desirable difficulties to enhance learning. In M. A. Gernsbacher and J. Pomerantz (Eds.), *Psychology and the real world: Essays illustrating fundamental contributions to society (2nd edition)* (pp. 59-68). New York, NY: Worth Publishers.

[2] Soderstrom, N. C., & Bjork, R. A. (2015). Learning versus performance: An integrative review. *Perspectives on Psychological Science, 10,* 176-199.

[3] Brown, P. C., Roediger, H. L., III, & McDaniel, M. A. (2014). *Make it stick: The science of successful learning.* Cambridge, MA: Harvard University Press.

[4] Carey, B. (2015). *How we learn: The surprising truth about when, where, and why it happens.* New York, NY: Random House.

[5] Didau, D. (2015). *What if everything you knew about education was wrong?* United Kingdom: Crown House Publishing.

Chapter 1: Develop a Growth Mindset

[1] Dweck, C. S. (2006). *Mindset: The New Psychology of Success*. New York, NY: Random House.

[2] Ericsson, K. A., Krampe, R. Th., & Tesch-Römer, C. (1993). The role of deliberate practice in the acquisition of expert performance. *Psychological Review, 100,* 363-406.

[3] Paunesku, D., Walton, G., Romero, R., Smith, E.,Yeager, D., & Dweck, C. S. (2015). Mind-set interventions are a scalable treatment for academic underachievement. *Psychological Science, 26,* 784-793.

[4] Duckworth, A. L., Peterson, C., Matthews, M. D., & Kelly, D. R. (2007). Grit: Perseverance and passion for long-term goals. *Journal of Personality and Social Psychology, 92,* 1087-1101.

[5] Mueller, C. M. & Dweck, C. S. (1998). Intelligence praise can undermine motivation and performance. *Journal of Personality and Social Psychology, 75,* 33-52.
See also:
Dweck, C. S. (2007, December). The secret to raising smart kids. *Scientific American Mind, 18*(6). Retrieved from http://www.scientificamerican.com/article/the-secret-to-raising-smart-kids/.

Chapter 2: Put Yourself to the Test

[1] Roediger, H. L., III, & Karpicke, J. D. (2006). Test-enhanced learning: Taking memory tests improves long-term retention. *Psychological Science,* 17, 249-255.

[2] Landauer, T. K., & Bjork, R. A. (1978). Optimum rehearsal patterns and name learning. In M. M. Gruneberg, P. E. Morris, & R. N. Sykes (Eds.), *Practical aspects of memory* (pp. 625-632). London: Academic Press.

[3] Murphy Paul, A. (2015, August). Researchers find that frequent tests can boost learning. *Scientific American, 313*(2). Retrieved from http://www.scientificamerican.com/article/researchers-find-that-frequent-tests-can-boost-learning/.
See also these companion papers:
Roediger, H. L., Agarwal, P. K., McDaniel, M. A., & McDermott, K. B. (2011). Test-enhanced learning in the classroom: Long-term improvements from quizzing. *Journal of Experimental Psychology: Applied, 17,* 382-395.
McDaniel, M. A., Agarwal, P. K., Huelser, B. J., McDermott, K. B., & Roediger, H. L. (2011). Test-enhanced learning in a middle school science classroom: The effects of quiz frequency and placement. *Journal of Educational Psychology,* 103, 399-414.

[4] Carey, B. (2014, September). Why flunking exams is actually a good thing. *The New York Times Magazine*. Retrieved from http://www.nytimes.com/2014/09/07/magazine/why-flunking-exams-is-actually-a-good-thing.html.

Chapter 3: Space It Out

[1] Ebbinghaus, H. (1964). *Memory: A contribution to experimental psychology* (H. A. Ruger, C. E. Bussenius, & E. R. Hilgard, Trans.). New York, NY: Dover Publications. (Original work published 1885)

[2] Budé, L., Imbos, T., van de Wiel, M. W., & Berger, M. P. (2011). The effect of distributed practice on students' conceptual understanding of statistics. *Higher Education, 62,* 69-79.

[3] Bahrick, H. P. (1979). Maintenance of knowledge: Questions about memory we forgot to ask. *Journal of Experimental Psychology: General, 108,* 296-308.

[4] Cepeda, N. J., Pashler, H., Vul, E., Wixted, J. T., & Rohrer, D. (2006). Distributed practice in verbal recall tasks: A review and quantitative synthesis. *Psychological Bulletin, 132,* 354-380.

Chapter 4: Mix It Up

[1] Hall, K. G., Domingues, D. A., & Cavazos, R. (1994). Contextual interference effects with skilled baseball players. *Perceptual & Motor Skills, 78,* 835-841.

[2] Rohrer, D., & Taylor, K. (2007). The shuffling of mathematics problems improves learning. *Instructional Science, 35,* 481-498.

[3] Kornell, N., & Bjork, R. A. (2008). Learning concepts and categories: Is spacing the enemy of induction? *Psychological Science, 19,* 585-592.

Chapter 5: Keep It Fresh

[1] Kerr, R., & Booth, B. (1978). Specific and varied practice of motor skill. *Perceptual & Motor Skills, 46,* 395-401.

[2] Smith, S. M., Glenberg, A. M., & Bjork, R. A. (1978). Environmental context and human memory. *Memory & Cognition, 6,* 342-353.

[3] Smith, S. M., & Rothkopf, E. Z. (1984). Contextual enrichment and distribution of practice in the classroom. *Cognition and Instruction, 1,* 341-358.

[4] Goode, M. K., Geraci, L., & Roediger, H. L. (2008). Superiority of variable to repeated practice in transfer on anagram solution. *Psychonomic Bulletin & Review, 15*, 662-666.

Chapter 6: Explain Yourself

[1] Pressley, M., McDaniel, M. A., Turnure, J. E., Wood, E., & Ahmad, M. (1987). Generation and precision of elaboration: Effects on intentional and incidental learning. *Journal of Experimental Psychology: Learning, Memory, and Cognition, 13*, 291-300.

[2] Woloshyn, V. E., Pressley, M., & Schneider, W. (1992). Elaborative interrogation and prior-knowledge effects on learning of facts. *Journal of Educational Psychology, 84,* 115-124.

[3] Smith, B. L., Holliday, W. G., & Austin, H. W. (2010). Students' comprehension of science textbooks using a question-based reading strategy. *Journal of Research in Science Teaching, 47*, 363-379.

[4] Berry, D. C. (1983). Metacognitive experience and transfer of logical reasoning. *Quarterly Journal of Experimental Psychology, 35A*, 39-49.

Chapter 7: Teach It to Learn It

[1] Cohen, P. A., Kulik, J. A., & Kulik, C. C. (1982). Educational outcomes of tutoring: A meta-analysis of findings. *American Educational Research Journal, 19,* 237-248.

[2] Roscoe, R. D., & Chi, M. T. H. (2007). Tutor learning: The role of explaining and responding to questions. *Instructional Science, 36*, 321-350.

[3] Nestojko, J. F., Bui, D. C., Kornell, N., & Bjork, E. L. (2014). Expecting to teach enhances learning and organization of knowledge in free recall of text passages. *Memory & Cognition, 42,* 1038-1048.

Chapter 8: Look Back to Move Forward

[1] Soderstrom, N. C., Clark, C., Halamish, V., & Bjork, E. L. (2015). Judgments of learning as memory modifiers. *Journal of Experimental Psychology: Learning, Memory, and Cognition, 41,* 553-558.

[2] Payne, J. D., Tucker, M. A., Ellenbogen, J. M., Wamsley, E.J., Walker, M. P, Schacter, D. L., & Stickgold, R. (2012). Memory for semantically related and unrelated declarative information: The benefit of sleep, the cost of wake. *PLoS ONE, 7.*

Chapter 9: Imagine That

[1] Leutner, D., Leopold, C., & Sumfleth, E. (2009). Cognitive load and science text comprehension: Effects of drawing and mentally imagining text content. *Computers in Human Behavior, 25,* 284-289.

Chapter 10: Visualize Your Path to Success

[1] Haefner, J. (n.d.) Mental rehearsal & visualization: The secret to improving your game without touching a basketball! Retrieved from https://www.break-throughbasketball.com/mental/visualization.html.

[2] Pham, L. B., & Taylor, S. E. (1999). From thought to action: Effects of process- versus outcome-based mental simulations on performance. *Personality and Social Psychology Bulletin, 25,* 250-260.

Photographs and Illustrations

Shutterstock image 10377628 of Boy holding books by Jason Stitt; image 36917170 of Wooden puzzle by Alexey Lebedev; image 36917176 of Wooden puzzle by Alexey Lebedev; image 36943816 of Wooden puzzle by Alexey Lebedev; image 51046636 of White podium by Bioraven; image 74220652 of Young Indian female student studying by Arek Malang; image 78773269 of Asian college student with lapto[p by Arek Malang; image 84443560 of Student with books on the head by Aaron Amat; image 85121002 of Red hair female student using a tablet by Wave Break Media; image 86443315 of Royal wedding breakfast by Georgios Kollidas; image 91798808 of Young teenager looking up by Ostill; image 95996329 of Multiple choice examination by Levent Konuk; image 99690071 of Young teenager with smart phone by Ostill; image 100740637 of Red hair young man thinking by Ollyy; image 101161744 of Blue thought bubble by Godruma; image 103783655 of Young man using a mobile phone by Ollyy; image 103783664 of Composition of student in different activity by Ollyy; image 104756429 of Student in library by Lightpoet; image 110919260 of Hispanic student sitting by Arek Malang; image 113158468 of Black and white seamless background by Magenta10; image 117058162 of Pencil ribbon banner by FeelPlus; image 126952172 of Male African American student in library by Michael Jung; image 127389608 of Human brain tree metaphor by art4all; image 128292047 of Female African American student sitting in lecture room by Michael Jung; image 133805588 of Student raising hands by Robert Kneschke; image 135053879 of Photocomposite of human brain by Agsandrew; image

140831617 of student doing research in library by Minerva Studio; image 146083217 of Students in computer lab by goodluz; image 150503795 of Speech balloons by Loshi Losh; image 150587642 of Top view of two students by Bikeriderlondon; image 157244387 of Red vintage car by Vladimir Arndt; image 159645998 of DNA molecule by Palau; image 169905173 of Baseball players to practice pitching outside by Tom Wang; image 171261476 of Dog in glasses reads red book by Igor Normann; image 195723236 of I love ink stamp by Thomas Pajot; image 197705363 of Vintage clouds by Flas 100; image 205425871 of Hexagon pin pointer by Hluboki Dzianis; image 209829898 of Girl shooting basketball by Oleg Mikhaylov; image 209829922 of Sporty girl dribbling a basketball by Oleg Mikhaylov; image 218227201 of Asian student doing homework by Dragon Images; image 221470261 of Wire-frame human face by Agsandrew; image 223024792 of Striped loopy tape seamless background by Curly Pat; image 223918066 of Teacher with college students by Monkey Business Images; image 224858431 of Striped hexagon seamless pattern by Curly Pat; image 225949720 of Striped triangles seamless pattern by Curly Pat; image 232184560 of Man showing time on clock by file404; image 232190926 of Man looks at magazine by file404; image 234356509 of 15-min stopwatch symbol by Blan-k; image 235520458 of Woman climbing rock wall by Proprotskly Alexey; image 237272356 of Group of people in the form of an arrow by Tai11; image 242729950 of Monochrome braids seamless background by Curly Pat; image 243250798 of Woman thinking green by Retrorocket; image 243253846 of Corporate ladder business people by Retrorocket; image 243318520 of Home in a maze by Retrorocket; image 244867228 of Striped rhombuses seamless background by Retrorocket; image 247531369 of Path to succerss illustration by Retrorocket; image 247830844 of Wavy graphic backgound by Curly Pat; image 247840396 of Profile and front illustration by Ollyy; image 249254671 of Infographic of brain learning by FeelPlus; image 249255574 of Pencil head illustration by FeelPlus; image 250207951 of Monochrome linear waves background by Curly Pat; image 261177638 of Pop-Up book graphic by FeelPlus; image 264406220 of Group of students studying by GaudLab; image 264717053 of Molecular DNA model by Alice-Photo; image 269430476 of Hispanic teenage girl looking up by Samuel Borges; image 272910527 of Group of people in the form of square with arrows by Tai11; image 272953844 of Fractal blue circle illustration by Fernando Batista; image 275614892 of 3D Cone wireframe element by AntartStock; image 295892561 of White marble head of young woman by Gilmanshin; image 296098034 of Polyonal linear grid striped pattern by Curly Pat; image 312177788 of seamless monochrome striped cube pattern by Supermimicry; image 325356566 of DNA molecule background by Palau; image 331144637 of Inscription of question mark on sweaty glass by Alina Re-viakina; image 341323505 of Human digestive organs by Chombosan; image 346099505 of Sphere wireframe by Yuliya Korchevska; image 354272660 of A pencil sitting on test bubble sheet by Vixit; image 355915094 of Tired student with book by Eldar Nurkovic; image 357424331 of Calendar page background by Evlakhov Valeriy; image 364050461 of Young male hip hopper by Luckyraccoon; image 367485941 of Paper speech bubble by Anna Fomina; image 370362275 of Solar system icon by Marnikus; image 371590864 of Neon transparent wave lines background by Kstudija; image 371590882 of Neon trans-parent wave lines background by Kstudija; image 212576893 of Germany tourist attrac-tion icons by Macrovector; and image 226219396 of Canada tourist attraction icons by Macrovector are works copyrighted by their respective artists and photographers.

CPSIA information can be obtained
at www.ICGtesting.com
Printed in the USA
LVOW05s2334090616
491988LV00005B/6/P